14 Pictures of the Bench

Edited by

Margarita Bokshtein

2019

NAU LAB Publishing books may be purchased in bulk at special discounts for sales promotion, corporate gifts, fundraising, or educational purposes. Special edition can also be created to specifications. For details, contact the Publishing Department at stories@naulab.pro

CHAPTER I.

Judicial Functions.

A common error is the supposition that a judge is called upon to discharge a function of Deity. This has surrounded the occupants of the bench with an imaginary blaze of glory and has often tended to puff them up and intimidate those who have business with them. This supposition comes from a confusion of ideas, which a little clear thinking will dissipate.

The judge is neither the Creator nor Preserver of things human or divine. His business is to judge, to decide, to compare and determine relative to existing things. The same function is exercised by the person who identifies a calf, a section corner, a counterfeit bill, a piece of ore, or anything about which a dispute has arisen. The fact that a judge should separate the true from the false and declare the law does not change the character of his task. The parties furnish proof of what they claim the truth to be. He picks out the truth.

They furnish evidence of what they claim the law to be. He picks out the law. He acts according to rules made for him. If he weighs the evidence he acts as a scales. In measuring he is a yardstick. He must not add anything to the weight or the quantity. His mind should be so free from prejudice that it will respond readily, like a well-oiled balance. His yardstick must always be of the same length.

The justice which he administers does not emanate from him. If it is legal justice the law has already determined it. If it is justice arising from the nature of things the law of nature has fixed it. Any self-interest or other bias tending to incline his mind in favor of one party or the other unfits him for his task. It falsifies his judgment. If he mistakes his calling for that of a lawmaker or substitutes his own conscience for the mandates of the law or the proofs of facts, he is a false balance, an elastic yardstick, a cheating device.

Our government is divided into three branches —legislative, executive and judicial. The first makes the laws, the second declares them and the third enforces them. The splendid super structure of our liberties is supported by these three pillars. The proper balance can only be maintained by each department attending strictly to its own business.

When a judge attempts to pass upon the justice of the law and modify it to suit his notions the legislature is put out of business. If he concludes the law is unjust and should not be enforced and so refuses to enter the judgment which the facts warrant, out of mercy for the culprit, the executive department is deprived of its function.

All questions as to what the law ought to be belong to the legislature. All relative to the execution of the sentence should be left to the executive department. The conscience of the judge should find satisfaction in the discharge of his judicial duties according to law. A violation of this rule abolishes government by law and substitutes government by caprice.

In such a government there would be greater uncertainty than at present. There would be as many laws as there are shades of opinion among judges. A judicial oligarchy would be established. It is ever the tendency of power to extend itself. If we concede that any judge, however honest and conscientious he may be, shall be permitted to deviate from the existing laws to satisfy his own notion of what the law ought to be, we establish a principle under which judges of less or no conscience will find excuse to act and thus make the tribunals of the law instruments to accomplish their own wills.

The safety of the republic demands imperatively that every occupant of the bench clearly understand the limit of his functions; that any deviation, however slight, for the purpose of effecting his own notions of justice, be considered a usurpation of power in the direction of tyranny; and that such judicial conduct be not tolerated or condoned by any motive, however meritorious.

The truth of the foregoing assertions is so plain that it must be conceded, and yet we hear on every hand stories of victories won by fervent oratory and brilliant wit, of the influence of friends, of the power of the press, of the pull of the politician.

Can any kind of oratory stretch a yardstick? May pathos increase the size of a bushel measure? What kind of wit can transform two into three or alter to any extent a real fact? How can the potent press or politician change the meaning of words? Is it any part of the function of the judge to decide who has the smartest lawyer or which suitor possesses the best character? Ought not the purest saint and the meanest corporation weigh the same in the judicial scales where the matter in controversy and not the character of the parties is at stake? Can three feet make more than a yard, whether the measurement be for a god or a devil?

Strictly speaking the judicial tribunal is hardly a fit place for rhetoric. It should be a forum for the accurate statement of facts, often as dry as dust except to those personally concerned. The rules of evidence should be devices to bring out these facts. The judge should be a magnet to attract the truth.

The luster of his countenance should illumine the dark places. His eyes should be keen to detect falsehood when masquerading in the guise of truth, and able to recognize the truth, even when mixed with falsehood. His ears should be quick to distinguish between the trembling accents of innocent modesty and the halting sentences of the false witness who is speaking his piece. He should have an internal perception that enables him to feel a liar, even though he has tricked himself out in all the habiliments of truth, and by which he can sense the true and honest witness even though circumstances have conspired to give him the appearance of fraud.

He must be able to sit with the judges of the loftiest courts and extract from their opinions the very substance of the points decided and take the place of the law writers in their studies and from their points of view get the real gist of their treatises. He should have the mental grasp that can collect within its scope the components of the legislature and extract from the mass the real meaning which is intended to be embodied in the law. From his place on the bench he should explore with the telescope of a fully informed mind the currents of jurisprudence, even to their fountain heads, and with the microscope of a trained and accurate judgment be able to tell exactly the nature of the thing presented to him for his decision.

The notion has somehow come into vogue that any person who has a license to practice law possesses the necessary qualifications for the bench. When, where, or under what circumstances this license was obtained is not usually inquired into. During the last quarter of a century diplomas from a multitude of colleges and universities have been issued to a great number of students, who, after a few months' attendance, are turned loose on the community armed with certificates under the seal of a corporation certifying that they are learned in the law.

The judges of courts in the various States have also with slight or no examination licensed large numbers of young and middle-aged men to practice law. It is safe to say that not one in ten of those thus graduated or licensed have knowledge sufficient to qualify for judicial positions. It is also certain that many years of study and experience in the actual trial and management of cases are necessary before the best educated student will possess such knowledge of the laws governing the rights of persons and property, the rules of evidence, and of pleading and practice as to equip him for the bench.

The general public have no means of ascertaining nor do they care to inquire whether the judicial aspirant has had this experience. What information they obtain on this subject they get from lawyers and the general reputation and standing of the candidate in the community. This is meager and unreliable, and the door has been opened through which many unlearned and incompetent men have been en abled to reach the bench with no proof of fitness except this license to practice. This is a public calamity, yet there are matters more important than learning to be taken into account.

The judge, incompetent for lack of legal knowledge and experience when elected, may acquire afterward in years of experience as a judge sufficient learning to fit him for the further discharge of his duties and the public who have educated him at great expense to themselves may at last reap the reward of patience. But far different are the defects in mental poise that retard the performance of judicial tasks. If the judge when first elected is disqualified by conceit, temper, lack of conscience, or other defects in disposition, he is likely to grow worse as the years go by. These defects, therefore, I consider of the most importance and present them first to your consideration.

CHAPTER II.

Egotism.

Judging is an act of intellect. It is an application of knowledge within to information without. Anything clogging the avenues of his in formation incapacitates the judge. Egotism is one cause of disqualification. The atmosphere surrounding the judicial office is calculated to stimulate conceit, especially in a young and in-experienced person. This office is no place for boys.

The judge sees before him men of advanced years, large experience and great reputation, pleading for persons who submit to him the decision of their causes. The judge sees before him men of advanced years, large experience and great reputation, pleading for persons who submit to him the decision of their causes. This spectacle is likely to give the youth an extravagant notion of his powers. If he, at his age, can occupy such a lofty eminence, he concludes that he is a superior being. This trait is further stimulated by the adulation of the cunning, who flatter his vanity to win his favor.

So subtle is conceit that no age is exempt. The veteran lawyer of large experience may be likewise badly disqualified. The successful practitioner who recalls his many victories and forgets his defeats, and in the fierce contest for patronage has collected a host of clients who frequently come to him for counsel, naturally acquires an inflated estimate of his knowledge and skill.

If elevated to the bench he considers his elevation a confirmation of this high estimate and begins at once to strut and treat with discourtesy the members of his profession. He becomes self-conscious and thinks of himself instead of the things which it is his duty to consider and prevents those who come before him from giving him the information which he should have if he is to judge correctly. As an illustration showing the effect of egotism on this office, consider the following:

Judge Knowall.

Many suitors with their attorneys and witnesses are waiting.
The jury are on hand, but Judge Knowall is late this morning.

Had any juryman been tardy the judge, if present, would have reprimanded or fined him. The lateness of a suitor or his attorney would have resulted in a judgment against him. But Judge Knowall comes when he gets ready—when he feels like it. None can tell exactly where this judge acquired his legal learning.

Certainly, he had not imperiled his health poring over musty volumes. He has evolved it from his inner consciousness. When he wishes to know anything, he goes to sleep and dreams it, or has a fit, and it comes to him. He picks nuggets of wisdom from the passing clouds.

How he became a member of the bar is not certain. He may have been a halfback in football team at some law college and graduated as a mere incident. Perhaps he gave banquet to the judges and someone moved his admission to the bar and the motion carried unanimously. Possibly he stumbled against a copy of Blackstone and absorbed it by juxtaposition.

Such a genius never suffers the tedious labor necessary to become lawyer. If he is a self-made man, he made himself in a hurry. Like the blazing comet that causes all the stars to look pale as it passes, he took his flight sublime. When he wanted anything, he grabbed it, and he wanted everything he could get his hands on. Other men lacking self-confidence have modestly waited for an invitation to run for office.

Sure of his fitness for everything, he has been a standing candidate for every office and many office at the same time. In clubs, social, civil and military, churches, boards, and every other conceivable form of organization which contains a prominent place where the occupant can either pose or draw salary, he has pushed were salary, he has pushed himself to the front.

In an evil hour he aspired to the bench, allured by the salary and opportunity for display. The glare that accompanies such assurance attracts voters as the arc light draws bugs and flies. Most people admire quick action, and the egotist drives everything before him with haste. His rough-and-tumble, slam-bang, knockdown-and-drag-out methods bring a large following. Even the man run over by this rough-rider will get up, dig the dirt out of his eyes and join the crowd. Let an egotist declare himself a god and he will always find followers ready to fight for him and empty their wallets into his hands.

The cause of the tardiness of Judge Knowall is uncertain. The game of draw-poker the night before may have been unusually interesting. On his way to the courtroom he may have been sidetracked by a chum or horse-shredded by a politician. If any form of reading matter has caused his delay it was not legal literature.

At last there is a rustle of excitement in the crowd and Judge Knowall appears clothed in thunder. He is a tall, angular man, straight as an arrow, with high cheekbones, a closely cropped and bristly beard, and stiff hair which stands on his head like the bristles of a scrubbing-brush. His cheeks are sunken, and many irregular wrinkles play criss-cross on his rugged features. His thin lips and firm-set mouth open and shut like a steel trap. The half-moons under his sunken eyes and bushy eyebrows present a brown and baggy appearance. His strong nose, nubby at the end, has some of the color which the rest of his countenance lacks and looks as if it could snort fire at any time.

This man is certainly intended to stir up things and make other people stand around and await his pleasure. He has a reckless audacity, will dip into and take charge of anything. Like the bold corsair of the deep, he strides into the court-room and takes his place upon the bench, and after an announcement by the bailiff he begins to call his docket.

"Jury in the box!" he exclaims. Twelve demure-looking captives of the law take their places on the hard wood furniture. "Examine the jury," exclaims the judge.

A frightened lawyer rises meekly and starts to state his case and ask some questions, when the judge interrupts and attempts to tell the jury what the case is about.

"Gentlemen," he asks, "do you know anything about this case, the parties or the attorneys?"
In answer to this the jury look stupid and express their ignorance. The judge says, "Here is a fair jury, gentlemen,

proceed with the trial unless you have some further question or challenge to make."

With a feeling of suppression, the plaintiff's attorney puts a witness on the stand and begins to examine him. Judge Knowall stops the attorney and proceeds to both examine and cross-examine the frightened witness. The lawyers on both sides sit cowed and silent spectators.

When the judge has finished with the plaintiff's witnesses, he may instruct the jury to find for the defendant, or he may play the same examination game with the defendant's witnesses. He exhibits throughout an appalling ignorance of the rules of evidence.

If objection is made it is immediately overruled. If the attorney persists the Supreme Court once decided in favor of his position, the judge says, "Pass up the book." He looks at the cover, squints at the syllabus, says he knows all about it, and tells the attorney to take his exception and give the Supreme Court a chance to guess again.

If the victim of this arbitrary abuse of power ventures to talk back and call attention to the expense an appeal will cause his client, he provokes a tirade of sarcasm and vituperation from the bench. On one occasion I heard such a judge launch against meek, bald barrister the following: "Sit down there, sit down, I say, or I'll retire you from general circulation. A little animated specimen of imbecility who has scratched all the hair off his head trying to hunt an idea must not insult this court after it has rendered its decision." In this summary and reckless manner, the fortunes, liberties, and perhaps the lives of the citizens of the republic are put in jeopardy and disposed of as if they were garbage on their way to the scrap heap.

Such a judge holds court as if it were a slave pen, feels none of the responsibility of his position, and cares but little for the consequences of his acts. He clears his docket in short order and uses his judicial position as a steppingstone to some office of still greater salary. The general public rarely learn how their power is abused. The lawyers know of it, but they endure it without public complaint, often fearing the consequences that may come to them from the ill-will of such a judge. Such is the havoc that egotism plays when permitted to exercise judicial functions.

As captain of industry or a military chieftain Judge Knowall would be a shining success. Those qualities which fit him for such pursuits unfit him for the bench. It is most essential that the judge should know his dependence upon the bar for his information, and that there no lawyer so unlearned and inexperienced that he cannot tell the wisest judge things about the evidence and law in controversy that the judge does not know and not likely to ascertain from any other source.

An overbearing, arbitrary and conceited judge can get but little aid from the lawyers he intimidates. The man who modestly admits his ignorance and shows an eager desire to learn gets the greatest aid from attorneys, par ties, and witnesses.

CHAPTER III.

Courtesy.

Among civilized people courtesy is current coin. Savage tribes and even beasts appreciate it. It is the essence of the golden rule, the hand maiden of love. Without it no association can be pleasant, no home can be happy. The cross, crabbed, and ill-natured exhale the psychic influences of discomfort and confusion. From every portion of their bodies fly invisible arrows which tend to distract, confuse and undo all with whom they come in contact.

The true and refined, who have the purest purposes, are often injured more than the false and malicious. There is no place among civilized men where this pernicious influence can work greater harm than in a court of justice. The countenance of the judge should be illumined by kindness. All he does should bear the indelible stamp of a just purpose. This all must admit. Yet how frequently have judges lacked these qualities. As a sample of a discourteous judge, I present the following:

Judge Wasp.

It was commonly reported that when Judge Wasp was born, he had a complete set of teeth and that the first cry he uttered was a snarl. At a later period, his teeth projected, one setting farther out than the others, causing a malicious curve in one side of his thin upper lip. From his mother he inherited dyspepsia; from his father biliousness. By his habits of life he added to his inheritance several other diseases which became chronic, so that all his internal organs were quarreling with each other.

Every hair on his body pricked him like the quills of a porcupine. He was as lean as a hyena and as sallow as saffron. His thin nose was a beak. His piercing gray eyes glared upon you with an expression of mingled curiosity and contempt. When on the bench he was as stiff and solemn as an effigy upon the totem pole of a Digger Indian.

His voice had a thin nasal twang. It was a cross between the screech of a wild goose and the scraping of a stovepipe. He had a microscopic eye for flaws and defects and took a fiendish delight in finding fault with everybody and everything.

The character of his comments was bitter irony and sarcasm. His thrusts stung like poisoned arrows. His leisure was spent in searching the archives of law and literature for venomous matter. He had a keen relish for scandal and could collect more inside facts relative to the misdeeds of public men than any of his associates.

Each disreputable fact he considered a choice morsel and waited for an opportunity when his victim would be the most vulnerable and then impaled him with a solar plexus thrust. While at the bar he was in his element in cross-examination. Before he began a cross-examination, he would stare at the witness for a moment, his piercing eyes rapidly kindling into a blaze. The veins of his face and neck would swell with ire like the head of a coiled snake when ready to spring. His voice would take on such a tone of sarcasm and suspicion that the innocent witness would imagine that he sat before the Great White Throne and one of the imps of Satan had come to expose him and drag him down to torment.

The malevolent cloud which he raised was so great that every onlooker at once concluded the witness was a perjurer. Even the witness himself, although he knew that he had told the truth, could scarcely credit his own story. He was very strong in the prosecution of persons and in the defense of corporations. He was able to make the accused person feel so guilty and the corporation appear so innocent that the jury would convict one and acquit the other.

The talents of Judge Wasp brought him a large practice and his services were widely sought. In a suit where there was much malice, he was a desirable mouthpiece, and even if his client were defeated the enjoyment the client experienced in hearing the opposite party abused made him willing to pay a large fee.

The interests which Judge Wasp had so long represented at the bar finally placed him on the bench. After he became a judge no one, from the judges of the Supreme Court down to the bailiff, could escape the venom of his tongue. At every stage of the proceedings of a case before him he found opportunity to lampoon or lacerate some attorney, party, witness, or bystander. He kept the atmosphere about the bench streaked with sulphur.

I was personally acquainted with such a judge. Here are some of his remarks which I have treasured in memory:

Of a certain witness he said: Ananias and Saphira were struck dead for lying; how this man and his wife live I cannot understand."

In a contest over a piece of land he said of one of the parties: "If I had forty acres and this man wanted it, I would deed it to him and save him the trouble of swearing me out of it."

Of another witness he said: "If he has a truthful countenance, God Almighty cannot write a legible hand."

In divorce suit brought by an attorney he said to the plaintiff when granting the decree: "I congratulate you on finding out by the aid of a detective what everybody knew."

An attorney made an objection and was about to amplify it. "Pass on to the next point," snarled the judge; "I fully understand that."

When the attorney persisted in arguing the point, he said: "You have nothing further to say; sit down." The lawyer's face turned red and he dropped to his seat.

The judge said: "Are you beginning to see yourself as others see you?"

A lawyer was defending a liquor dealer in a suit brought for unlawful sale of intoxicating liquors. The judge compared the intoxicated man to a starved sucker, the saloon keeper to a bloodsucker on his neck, and the attorney of the saloonkeeper to a little blood sucker on the big blood-sucker.

To another attorney he said: "Is it possible for the court to put an idea into your head without a surgical operation?"

To another he said: "Don't get it into your head that you know any law, for you do not. If a legal proposition should enter into your cranium it would kill you as quick as a stroke of lightning."

On another occasion he said to a lawyer: "It's a pity that a fellow who has brass enough to get lawsuits hasn't brains enough to try them."

Referring to a certain witness, he said: "I am inclined to believe in the transmigration of souls, that when one per son dies and another is born, the soul passes from the dead man to the new-born babe, but I think when this man was born nobody died."

Referring to the testimony of an expert witness, he remarked: "It is written in Scripture that the ox knoweth his owner and the ass his master's crib."

Once he had a bystander arrested for making a noise in court. After he had scolded him a few minutes, he said: "Were I not afraid of sending your family to the poorhouse, I would fine you fifty cents for contempt."

Such was the character of the emanations from Judge Wasp. Vitriol was mixed with everything he did. Everyone before him was in mortal terror. None knew whose turn would come next.

Lawyers were abashed and confused, dared not attempt arguments or take issue with the court on any question. Witnesses were frightened and their memories failed. The parties had no confidence in the judge and were glad to get their cases out of his court.

His is an extreme case but illustrates how essential to a judge is a good temper and a kind disposition. Exactly contrary should be the conduct of a judge. All concede that the judge *has a right to demand courtesy from everyone. This is neces-sary to avoid irritating him. If irritated his attention is dis-tracted and he becomes disabled. This applies with equal force to those who appear before him. No attorney can do his best before a judge who treats him with disrespect.*

Most lawyers, and inexperienced ones especially, are con-fused by offensive conduct on the part of the court. Remarks from the bench reflecting upon the demeanor or veracity of witnesses frighten and stupefy them. Such remarks impair the memory of the witnesses and prevent them from telling the truth when they most desire to.

The parties become panic-stricken and question the integrity of the judge. If unsuccessful they conclude that it is due to his corruption. The jury ate confused and bewildered by such conduct. The judge should strive to create an atmosphere most favor able to the comfort of himself and of those associated with him, and such as will aid and encourage all persons con-cerned to do their part in the best manner. If he cannot do this he is out of his place.

He may be the most learned lawyer in the land. He may have tried suits about every bone in the human body, and every kind of property. He may have defended and prosecuted every species of criminal charge and per-formed all these tasks with a great degree of skill. His services in his profession may command for him a salary much greater than that paid to him as a judge; but if he has a hateful disposition, is irascible and lacks the patience to treat everyone as he would wish to be treated, he is unfit to be a judge and is likely to become a common scold, a public nuisance, and bring the administration of justice into contempt.

The judicial office is therefore not the proper asylum for broken-down nervous systems, or for men who have failed in every other business on account of bad temper.

CHAPTER IV.

Concentration.

The nature of the mental process that takes place in forming a judgment requires a joint act of memory and decision. The things to be judged must be recalled and be present in the mind in order that they may be compared and examined, and their similarity or dissimilarity accurately ascertained. This requires time, in which the attention of the person who is forming the judgment must be concentrated to the task.

The judicial officer may have the learning and disposition and yet become so entangled with extraneous matters as to be deprived of the necessary concentration. To illustrate my meaning clearly, I will introduce a gentleman whose life was full of duties and desires that seriously interfered with the conduct of his court:

Judge Doall.

Judge Doall had a very industrious ancestry. His father was a blacksmith and his mother a poetess. His ancestors had been engaged in many different occupations. Among them had been distinguished boilermakers and music composers, butchers and florists, preachers and horse traders, elephant trainers and teachers of canary birds, astronomers and entomologists, poets and politicians. He inherited every talent and taste of which human nature is capable and had a passion for doing everything that anyone could do.

He was medium height, medium flesh, and all his various faculties developed to a medium extent. His complexion was a cross between blonde and brunette. All parts of his form and features were evenly developed and of medium size. The only thing extraordinary about him was that he had as much capacity for one thing as for another.

His all-around tastes and desires brought him into every field of action. He was well educated, and his education covered a vast range. The complicated Greek verb was a plaything. Egyptian hieroglyphics were as simple as Aesop's Fables. He read Sanskrit before breakfast. He carried most modern languages on his tongue's end.

He could tell the kind and quality of every liquor. He carried the knowledge of every science in his vest pocket. He could paint a picture or a barn. He knew the name of every constellation and all visible stars were familiar faces. He could play on the most difficult instruments. He could sing all forms of composition and reel gracefully in every kind of dance. He could write an epic poem or a pill advertisement. If at a funeral and the minister failed to arrive, he could deliver the sermon. If at an entertainment they desired a vaudeville stunt he could do anything from an acrobatic act to a fancy dance.

He was always ready to speak on any topic suggested and to undertake any task. His ability to do a great many things did not satisfy him. In order that his time might be fully employed every moment, he usually tried to do many things at the same time.

When elevated to the bench he was about fifty years of age; had been married five times and had thirteen living children. Four had perished prematurely.

His first wife was the buxom daughter of a Scotch washerwoman. She died of nervous prostration. His second, a teacher of physical culture, died of paresis. The third was square-shouldered, broad-headed and masculine, and lived with him long enough to have ten children, then left him in disgust after she had been several times bitten by his pet snake. He obtained a divorce from her. The fourth was a champion female walkist, but she soon found that she could not keep up with him and procured a divorce on the ground of cruel and inhuman treatment. The fifth was the widow of a prize fighter, but the judge soon knocked her out of the *ring, and after giving birth to a few children she took a safe place beside the first two in the cemetery. She died from a complication of diseases induced by his strenuous life.*

The first child that he lost was killed by the explosion of a new gas with which the judge was experimenting; the second was killed by falling from his arms on the stairway while he was ascending with and engaged in composing an exegesis on the "Deceitfulness of Riches." While carrying the third and watching the flight of a comet they both fell into well and the child was drowned. The fourth one was playing about while his father was moving a hen house and the house fell on it.

While thus trying to perform several tasks at the same time the judge had often received injuries to different portions of his body and had thus accumulated a glass eye. But these domestic and personal calamities did not take away his desire to do all the business in the world, nor keep him out of entanglements with the opposite sex.

Soon after the loss of his last wife he undertook a series of complicated courtships. He fascinated the president of "Female Single-Tax Club." She was a maiden lady so fat that her chin rested on her bosom. He charmed Christian Science healer who might have made a fortune for him as living skeleton. He was received with favor by the relict of a deceased hotelkeeper, who had continued the business successfully after her husband's death. Profoundly did he impress the heart of a dying-swan, bury-me-beneath-the weeping-willow poetess, who declared that the judge was a "song of love." These are but a few who enjoyed intermittently his dazzling smile.

Many were the business enterprises which he undertook. He operated a cheese factory, made sugar-coated pills, raised poultry, smoked hams, edited a newspaper, directed a female seminary, was president of a political club', knew every voter in his precinct, every prominent person in his ward, every political leader in his county, and was acquainted with all the party managers in the state and nation.

He had business enough without aspiring to be a judge, but he saw a chance to take that in as an incident to his manifold affairs, and so he did. Had he classified and systematized his extensive matters and conducted them by agents trained for departments, he might have succeeded better. But such a genius despises system and classification.

Judge Doall did everything haphazard. His pigeonholes were his pockets. Into these he crammed everything for which he had use. I will not attempt to enumerate all the articles that crowded these receptacles, but among them were a telescope, a microscope, a pair of shears, a box of pills, foreign and domestic correspondence, magazines, and works of science, art and literature, and a long pocketbook containing money, checks, receipts, cards and memoranda, and such other things as would reach him from day to day. When his pockets

bulged to overflowing, he emptied them into a drawer un as-
sorted.

When he wanted anything, he would dig into this drawer and
get what he could reach conveniently. Some letters he never
answered, some he answered twice, some were eaten up by
mice who nested in the drawer, others were worn into illegi-
bility before they reached the drawer.

His financial matters were conducted in the same loose man-
ner. He paid his bills on the street or anywhere he happened
to be, when he had the money, and but rarely paid them
when due or according to promise. He deposited his checks
when he remembered them, sometimes after they were full of
holes. He usually was late and often forgot his engagements,
not only the dates, but the nature of the business to be trans-
acted. Even the ladies he visited made frequent complaints
because he forgot his appointments with them.

He might start for church and stop at a minstrel show, quit
writing an ode to melancholy and do a buck and wing dance
or a hoe-down. Having dressed for a wedding, he might at
tend a funeral. Men in every walk of life were liable some
time during the day or night to meet the judge. How could a
person so entangled be expected to conduct a court on time?

Some days he was long waited for but did not come. On the
days he did arrive he was surrounded by a crowd of distract-
ing influences. It required great patience to try a case before
him. When you were introducing evidence to establish the

disputed boundary of a piece of land his mind might be among the pyramids or be composing an article on Chinese chess, or a comic song.

When you were arguing a constitutional question and you saw his eyes roll heavenward, you were not sure he was following you. Perhaps he was stringing together musical cadences or trying to invent a new process for flavoring cheese. When you were making a most fervid appeal for the redress of your client's wrongs, he often seemed as cold and unsympathetic as a granite tombstone.

He was not hearing you. He may at the time have been trying to decipher an inscription on a Babylonian tablet or trying to catch an unwary insect for examination by his new microscope. You were often interrupted to permit persons to speak to him relative to personal matters, and frequently was he called to his private room or the telephone.

No one who submitted to him a suit in the form of depositions could foretell when the judge would read them. If he did find time, he would only read two or three words on a page, take a run, jump through them, draw a long breath, guess and render his decision. He had birthdays, weddings, and funerals enough in his own family to seriously impair his usefulness, but these were few compared with the many that occurred among other relatives by blood or marriage.

***

The foregoing sketch of Judge Doall may be considered overdrawn, and perhaps it is, but every lawyer of court experience will recognize him. There are many men on the bench in this nation who had altogether too much business before they were elected and after assuming judicial duties have discharged them as mere incidents to their other affairs.

No lawyer can satisfactorily try a case before judge who does not give him his undivided attention, and no judge can properly hear a case and decide it who is being incessantly interrupted by thoughts and things foreign to the matter in controversy. The public should require of the occupant of the bench that he give to his great task that concentration and consecration which its importance re quires and deserves, and the man so situated that he cannot do this should not attempt to fill the office.

CHAPTER V.

Courage.

Much courage is often essential in the formation of a correct decision. The judge must have no master but the truth. At its shrine he must ever offer unswerving devotion. Very numerous are the influences employed to divert him from this. Some will seek to intimidate. If he can be terrified by threats either covert or open, powerful suitors, influential editors, and perhaps the unthinking mob will prevent him from accurately discharging his task.

It is essential that he have something in his breast that money cannot buy and an unfaltering courage that fears no consequences except such as can justly come from a failure to discharge his duty. Too often men are elevated to the bench who do not possess this courage.

There are some who bluff and bluster and give the impression that they are very firm and independent, but who have in fact "livers white as milk."

The really brave man does not put himself on dress parade. He does not hire a brass band and have his picture taken when he is about to do his duty, nor does he employ a press agent to advertise the act thereafter. Calmly and gently as the dew descends, he proceeds with his task, able without emotion to pit his individual thought against the clamors of the world. Such a man has metal for a good judge. The weak-kneed, time-serving lawyer is not fitted for the bench. I will illustrate this by another sketch:

Judge Fearful.

Judge Fearful was a born coward. He was frightened by the first glimpse he got of the earth and he never got over it. On a bright day he was afraid of sunburn. At night he trembled lest a shooting-star might hit him. He would not expose himself to a summer breeze lest he might take cold. He dreaded to draw a long breath for fear he might inhale a microbe. He never went out without an umbrella and gum shoes. A drop of moisture might injure him.

As a child he was "mother's boy," always did what he was told and stayed where he was put. At school he learned his lessons well and was not tardy or disobedient to his teacher. He had

*never used tobacco or intoxicating liquors or any other stim-
ulants. These he thought likely to injure his nerves and waste
his money. Outside the theater and music hall he heard the
song and dance, but he did not go in.*

*He might be contaminated by the gay throng. He was not in
sensible to the plump and rosy charms of the opposite sex,
but he yielded not, lest he might incur too great a responsibility. Nor did he poach upon the preserves of married men.
Once he was strongly tempted, but when he looked at the
statutes his pulse became normal and he got back into his
refrigerator.*

*When he had passed his prime and his eyelids had become
sticky and he was getting yellow under the ears, he met in a
business way the widow of an enterprising man who had left
her considerable property and several children. He concluded to step into the velvet shoes of the departed and administer the estate with widow and children annexed. In financial matters he was always prudent, saving a portion of
his small earnings and investing it in gilt-edged securities.
He shaved notes and drew interest on the shavings.*

*Ever keeping a weather eye for the main chance, he had his
sails closely reefed, carefully looking out for squalls and
storms. In politics he quietly followed the lead of the caucus
and convention, and in an unostentatious way voted the
ticket. He was always careful to keep in favor with the party
in power, but to also keep so near the border line as not to*

incur disfavor of the opposition. In religious matters he was careful to affiliate with the strongest church, making ample preparations for the burial of his body and the salvation of his soul.

In conversation he was a listener, never venturing an opinion unless asked, and then agreeing with the questioner, being careful to pump from the other party all the information that he could and at the same time impart none himself. He was a pessimist, ever anticipating and preparing for the worst, fearing that a volcano might burst under him or that the tail of a comet might sweep down from the heavens and destroy him.

He had a mind eager for statistics and accumulated much inside information relative to the forces about him, seeking always an alliance with the strongest force, yet he kept in the rear under cover, where there was the least danger from hostility. Scrupulously neat and fashionable in his attire, he was always polite in the extreme. Once when a horse kicked him he took off his hat and begged its pardon.

He especially courted the rich and powerful. His diet was simple. His blood had the consistency of skimmed milk. He wore a beard that might have been the envy of the god of war, but this pretentious excrescence did not indicate military courage. He was afraid his throat might be cut while being shaved and his pocketbook depleted at the same time. The fine lines upon his forehead and around his eyes were not formed by a strong determination in the path of duty.

There was no terror in his frown, even when he made a strong attempt to bluster, because the mud in the bottom of his eye was too apparent. There was no glint of steel in its glance. He was a conformist.

Like the tree-toad, he tried to take the color of the bark he was on and always tried to cling to the best bark. He lived in a city divided by a river, and there was a rivalry between those living on the east and those on the west side. If he located on the east side the people on the west side would oppose him, and vice versa. So, he finally acquired an island in the middle of the stream and built thereon.

When he met an east sider, he claimed to reside on the east side, and when he met a west sider he said he resided on the west side. At the bar he seldom tried a lawsuit, his first thought being to settle or compromise. Sometimes he made a show of courage to inspire some respect in his adversary, but the feeble cloud he exhibited soon showed its silver lining by an offer to split the difference.

His most valuable services were in surrounding and enmeshing the unwary delinquent debtor. He could ensnare a man in failing circumstances and creep over him like the ivy grows around the mouldering wall, profiting largely by his ruin. This he did so gently and with such affectation of piety and sweetness of temper that the man who slipped naked out of his clutch felt that the hand of Providence had been his un-doing and that Judge Fearful had saved him from a worse fate.

There came a time when political managers wanted a judge they could control easily, and they selected him for the bench. There he was always safe and sane. He never wandered far from the beaten paths. He showed charming patience in tri-als and listened to all that anyone cared to say. His influence was used to compromise the matter if possible. Otherwise he ascertained the stronger side or the one he feared the least and gave that the victory.

If the weaker appealed he was careful to make the record as strong as he could in favor of his opinion, and prevent the loser from securing a fair review in the upper court. A cham-pion prize fighter of world-renown once said to the writer that he would prefer to fight a brave man rather than a cow-ard, because, he said, "the coward is afraid to get near enough so that you can hit him, and if he gets the advantage of you he will kill you."

This judge was so much afraid that his decisions would be re-versed that it was difficult to get him to sign a true bill of ex-ceptions. Strong influences were brought to control him. He was controlled by some lawyers and that being generally known they obtained much patron age on account of it.

Newspaper editorials had great influence with him. He kept his ear to the ground for political earthquakes and listened for subterranean voices. In choice language he gently read from the black book of the law the hardest sentence against the poor and defenseless, but with plausible sophistry permitted the rich to escape.

He did not do this corruptly. He never took a bribe, nor did he make corrupt contracts. This conduct was due to the fact that from first to last he was an unmitigated coward, who dared not stand by his own opinion in the face of powerful opposition.

It would seem unnecessary to point out more particularly the pernicious effect of such a judge upon our civil and criminal jurisprudence. A just judicial system cannot rest on such a rotten foundation. The property, liberty, and lives of citizens must be guarded by law. It can afford no adequate protection if those who administer it are mere puppets, manipulated by designing persons, or weathercocks that point the way the popular wind blows. The constitution and the laws become wastepaper, if the officers who hold the scales of justice manipulate them like loaded dice.

CHAPTER VI.

Decision.

After the parties have had a fair hearing the judge must decide. To do this requires a mental force that some do not possess. They spend much time halting where the roads fork, unable to determine which path to take. Certain knowledge is often impossible and when we have all the information attainable by a reasonable investigation we must decide or forever halt. This requires the nerve that is essential in judicial proceedings. Lack of this power of decision seriously impairs the judicial officer. To illustrate this I introduce my friend

Judge Wabbler.

The Honorable Socrates Wabbler was intended by nature for a question mark. It was well for him that he was not permitted to choose whether he would be a boy or a girl. It would have taken him so long to have made the choice he would have been gray headed before he was born.

He was built on the principle of the curve. He was fat, bow-legged, round-headed, had puffed cheeks, could not walk straight, sit straight, or do anything in a direct way. His bones and muscles were small. It seemed as if his digestive organs were in doubt whether they should use nourishment for bones or muscles and being unable to decide had deposited great round lumps of fat on every portion of his body. The nearest approach to anything straight about him was his pug nose, which turned Heavenward as if to ask a solution of the riddle of the universe.

Under the broad brow of Judge Wabbler were more doubts than anyone could enumerate. No proposition could be stated that he did not question or advocate a modification. Not that he desired to be contrary. He only desired to get at the truth. Such were his habits of indecision and so great his fear of a mistake that he looked for both sides of the proposition and gathered all the facts. The hinges of his mind were so well oiled that after he had once decided he changed it with the greatest celerity and appeared to enjoy such a change.

He entered college to be educated for the ministry but because of his practice of doubting everything he was advised to become a lawyer and he followed the advice. Here he industriously searched for antique and obsolete precedents and curious reasons for doubting the rule written in the books or taught by the professors. This trait was manifested in his affairs of the heart. For a long time, he had visited a widow and her daughter and with equal affection for each. Finally, he arranged to marry the mother. On the day set he met a friend who congratulated him on his choice. This caused a change in his plan and he married the daughter, concluding that by doing so he would have the society of both.

His practice while at the bar was not large. When persons came to him for counsel, he suggested so many doubts, asked so many questions, wanted to make so much investigation and was so uncertain in his opinion that most people preferred to consult with a lawyer, who assumed to know more off-hand. The members of his profession, however, appreciated his modesty and his appetite for concrete facts and secured his election to the bench.

It required great patience to try a case before a judge who had so strong a desire for fundamentals, one who thought nothing fit to eat until he had first chewed it, and insisted upon going back to the fountain-head and examining with minuteness the inception of every doctrine asserted as law. He usually required each lawyer to make an oral argument and present a written brief. He then examined in detail the cases cited and searched for himself to find cases not so cited and any further knowledge that he could obtain to throw light upon the proposition.

He usually reached a decision a long time after he had taken the matter under advisement and then took delight in reversing himself. A very slight reason was sufficient to cause him to set aside his judgment.

It is said he spent four weeks in trying an action against a steamboat Company. The plaintiff claimed damage on account of scurvy contracted during a long voyage. A verdict was returned for the defendant. A new trial was asked for error in the Court's instructions. Seventy-five charges of negligence were made against the defendant in the furnishing and "failing to furnish proper food, in consequence of which plaintiff claimed he took the scurvy.

The Court had told the jury: "If the plaintiff has failed to prove any of the acts of negligence charged he cannot recover." The question arose on the meaning of the word "any." It was conceded that proof of one act was sufficient.

The plaintiff claimed the charge required him to prove all the seventy-five acts of negligence. The defendant insisted that the charge only required the proving of some one. The debate on the meaning of this word of three letters waxed hot and the investigations took a wide range. Dictionaries were searched, grammars were explored, sentences ancient and modern from approved authorities were cited and examined. All decisions reported in the English tongue were searched for parallels, and oral arguments of great length were made. These were full of enthusiastic appeals by the plaintiff's attorney, asking pity for his poor client so affected with the scurvy, and powerful admonitions by the defendant's counsel beseeching the Court not to allow the scurvy plaintiff to excite sympathy.

Elaborate briefs were filed. For many months was the case taken under advisement and deep did Judge Wabbler dig into the archives of antiquity for aid in deciding this momentous question. Finally, the attorneys were called into Court to hear his decision. He began to render it in his usual manner. In rendering a decision, he never used positive terms but usually said: "I incline to the view," or "my mind oscillates," or "my opinion seems to preponderate," etc.

When it became apparent that he was about to grant a new trial defendant's attorney started to his feet and begged leave to file further briefs. This the Court granted, stating that he was still in great doubt. Arrangement was then made for further briefs on both sides and again the Court took it under advisement.

After many more months of travail he again announced his readiness to deliver his decision. This time he was about to deny the motion and the plaintiff's attorney jumped to his *feet expressing his surprise and insisting that he be permitted to file further arguments. The Court granted the request, more briefs were filed, and further investigation made.*

After long consideration the Court again signified his readiness to deliver his opinion. When all had assembled again, he announced that he had decided to grant a new trial and started to give his reasons with great modesty and care.

The defendant's attorney interrupted the Court and began combating his reasons. So successful was he that the Court changed his mind again and announced his decision against a new trial. Then the plaintiff's attorney by a furious appeal assailed this action of the Court and the judge again took a position in his favor, and then plaintiff's counsel claimed that he was entitled to the last speech.

The question who was entitled to the last speech was then argued. After long discussion of his doubts the judge decided that the plaintiff was entitled to the last speech and that he should render his decision. The defendant's attorney then said: "What is your Honor's decision? You have made so many." Standing up and jerking his coat the judge said: "I have honestly and conscientiously tried to decide this motion and I have decided it, and I'll be damned if I will be further imposed upon." A dispute then arose between the attorneys as to how the Court had decided, and so great was the Judge's confusion that he had to turn to the Clerk and ask him what the last decision was he had rendered.

On another occasion when there was a very heated argument over the judge's ruling in a certain case and the defendant's attorney violently assailed it the plaintiff's attorney arose to re ply. The judge rising to his feet said: "Sit down, young man, I will answer this attorney myself." The judge then in a very forcible speech from the judge's bench sought to reply-to the defendant's argument. The plaintiff's attorney seeing that the judge was on his side greatly enjoyed the spectacle. But his enjoyment was short lived. When the judge had ceased his address, he turned to him and said: "Young man, I think we have beat him in the argument, but I fear he has got us on the facts."

Not only was a great quantity of arguments required by this judge, but a large number of questions had to be argued. In a case where a negro was indicted for burglary, charged with extracting a pullet from a hen roost, the settlement of the preliminary questions brought up many important contro- versies such as: Had the grand jury been legally drawn, were its members qualified, was the law constitutional, was the District Attorney qualified to prosecute, had he been elected, had the judge jurisdiction to hear the case, was the law under which he was elected constitutional, had it been properly adopted by the legislature?

So patient was this judge in this trial of this colored chicken- lifter that he sat for days investigating the question as to whether he should legislate himself out of office. Many of these questions were taken under advisement and considered on oral arguments and written briefs. At last the Court got to the question as to the sufficiency of the indictment. The letters "A. D." had been left off before the year of the date of the commission of the alleged burglary. The objection was made that the indictment was insufficient because it did not show whether the crime was committed before or after Christ. This was a poser. It was taken under advisement and held for so long a period that the prosecuting witness died and the other witnesses moved away and there was no one who could testify whether the crime was ever committed either during the Christian Era or prior thereto. Hence the suit was dismissed.

A suit was brought for divorce by Mrs. Smith against her husband. The judge after a long wrestling with the facts decided in favor of the lady, and entered a decree giving her a divorce. The attorney for Mr. Smith presented a petition for a re-hearing and filed a brief. The matter was taken under advisement by the Court and so remained for years. Finally, Mr. Smith became enamored of another lady and the parties agreed that the petition for a re-hearing be dismissed. Defendant's attorney, however, neglected to have the order entered. Supposing that proceedings were at an end both parties married again and had children. One day, years afterward, the Court ran onto this petition and brief where it had long lain overlooked and he discovered a point not previously raised by either party and granted the petition and set aside his decree. By this act both of the subsequent marriages became null and void, and bigamous, and the status of the children born since came into question. Mr. Smith died and in the probating of his estate the question arose whether the children born of the former Mrs. Smith during her second attempt at marrying could inherit Mr. Smith's property. These having been born during the existence of the marriage relation between Mr. and Mrs. Smith, it was contended, must be presumed in law to be Mr. Smith's children although the lady was at the time living with another man.

A breach of promise suit was brought by a lady against her recreant lover. So long did it take to reach a decision that before judgment could be obtained both parties had died, and the suit had to be carried on by the administrator of the plaintiff against the administrator of the defendant. It so continued until finally these administrators got together and adjusted the dam age to the heart of the deceased plaintiff by the broken contract of the deceased defendant on the basis of one-half of the estate left by him. One-half was taken by each party to pay the costs of suit and attorney's fees.

Judge Wabbler may be an extreme type but there are many judges in the United States so much like him that he will be quickly recognized. To such an extent does indecision or delay prevent the efficient administration of justice.

CHAPTER VII.

Vain Display.

Every creature takes delight in exhibiting it pelf. With what pride the peacock struts and displays his fine plumage. Likewise the Sioux chief fringes his head and spinal column with feathers. The Pharisee made long prayers in public places to be seen of men. For this reason the women deck themselves in all the colors of the rainbow. Behold the Shanghai rooster how he strides and flaunts his red comb to dazzle the hens of his flock. The bejeweled monarch in his robes of state acts on the same impulse. Some wear rings on their fingers, others bells on their toes.

The snake rattles his tail, and the danseuse her anklets. Here one enamels and plasters the face to present a smooth front, and there another is tatooed with the images of birds and animals. From the frozen zones to the tropical islands of equatorial seas all forms of life, human and animal, are engaged in decorating themselves. Even plants at certain seasons of the year put on blossoms of the most attractive colors to draw to their breasts the insects that bring the fertilizing pollen. The painter points with pride to his picture.

The fisherman exhibits his string of fish. To be observed men bravely endure the greatest perils by land and sea. It is this passion that makes heroes and martyrs. Even tyrants don themselves with blood-stained garments and usurp the thrones of power to attract the admiration of mankind. I do not condemn this passion. It has its proper place and uses. The acrobat may stand on his head for the amusement of the assembled audience, but it would not become a surgeon to assume such a position while performing an operation.

A Court of justice is not a circus and the judge should not try to play the clown or act as ring master. None of his energy should be expended in making a show of himself, for the energy so used is taken from the quantity that should be expended in doing his work. Many are the methods adopted by judges to put themselves on exhibition. A common one is to assume an oppressive and unnatural dignity. The king claims to be God's anointed and the holy oil drizzles from his head down to his justices and falls until it reaches the Justice of the Peace.

Every fellow touched by the sacred substance gets a petrified backbone and begins to talk out of his intestines. In dress and movements he strives to be different from his kind, thereby affecting a different nature. This stiff-necked and owl-like dignity has been developed in some Courts until the effect of it acts like a diuretic even on an experienced lawyer. Un less the judge has paralysis of the spinal and facial nerves this unnatural attitude cannot be maintained without much effort at acting, and the guttural monotones employed in the words he uses requires training and perpetual attention. This imposes a large amount of unnecessary labor upon the occupant of the bench and incapacitates those who come before him from con centration on the subject in hand.

Judicial dignity is only one of the various methods used in display. The judge in the rural district, clad in a threadbare suit, stained with dirt and victuals, who sits with his feet cocked upon the bench and squirts tobacco- juice on the stove, dropping a portion on his long beard, meanwhile telling a smutty story for the amusement of hangers-on, is trying just as hard to advertise himself as the judge who wears a wool wig and black alpaca kimona. But a few years ago, the population of the West depended upon the Courts for their entertainment.

When the judge and jurors came to the county seat the whole community was greatly stirred and the male portion crowded the filthy courtroom and remained during the entire session. There was then a great temptation for lawyers to appear smart and say and do things that attracted attention. The judge was usually infected with the disposition to show off and he vied with the lawyers in his efforts to dazzle the lookers-on.

If a judge had talent in this, his Court resembled a free vaudeville show where every kind of comedy and farce were presented. A very interesting event was the sentencing of the convict. Here the judge had his best opportunity for melodramatic display, and he worked it to the limit. A large part of the expenses of the trials were paid out of the public funds, and these shows, which were a small portion trial and a large part public entertainment, became very expensive luxuries to the taxpayers.

When not quite four years of age I witnessed a great public entertainment in the little town where I was born. For fifty miles men and women and children came in wagons, on horse-back and on foot. Many came the day before, sleeping on the ground and in sheds. Some travelled all night. For many hours a great multitude jostled and fought with each other to get choice places and when located stood through the long night, filling every available space about the plat form where this entertainment was to occur. Windows were rented and the roofs of houses and chimney tops were covered. Reserved seats were occupied upon the limbs of trees, where men and boys clung like swarms of bees, all eagerly waiting for the spectacle.

What attraction could pull this multitude from their homes? Was it some great orator, a reincarnation of the mighty Demosthenes, who was expected to speak upon the immortality of the soul? Was it some royal orchestra transported over the seas to entrance the people with the best music? Or were they expecting a second coming of the Messiah, or that Gabriel would appear and blow his famous trumpet? I doubt if any of these could have drawn such an eager and enthusiastic audience of old men, young men, maids, matrons, nursing babes, public officers and military companies. What did this vast aggregation come to see? A man killed! A common man! One with whom they had no acquaintance and in whom they had no special interest otherwise than to see him hanged.

From Maine to Texas the grass of the meadows and the weeds of the wilderness grow over the unknown graves of myriads of our country's sons who gave their lives in a struggle for human liberty. They expired as unnoticed as the spar row falls. And few have ever cared to learn their names or mark their graves. But so great was the interest in this judicial killing that whole counties were depopulated, and great trouble and expense incurred to see the horrible sight. The folly of such publicity in Court proceedings and the waste of time and tissue in thus conducting Court as a public show must be apparent to all.

I have known many judges to use their positions for the amusement of the public. Here is an example:

Judge Wind.

He died long ago, and when I look back upon his career through the misty past, I confess my inability to describe the characteristics about him that were so amusing. There was nothing unusual about his appearance. He had no grotesque features. He was tall, straight and well-proportioned. His forehead was broad and high, and his head thinly covered with dark hair. His face was long, cheek-bones high, and cheeks slightly sunken. His mouth and chin were regular. He sat on the bench in a natural manner, rarely smiled and never appeared as if trying to be funny or entertaining. Those who knew him loved him for the kindness of his heart and his manifest desire to temper justice with mercy.

He had a copious flow of language. His mind was so full of images, he expressed them in such glowing terms, they were so remote from the subject under discussion, he passed so rapidly from the sublime to the ridiculous, from the commonplace to the pathetic, he was animated with so great a number of disconnected and turbulent emotions, his remarks were so full of startling, trite and curious references, and all came forth with such profusion like liquid bursting out of an overcrowded cask, that it was impossible to listen to his effervescence without feeling an exhilaration and amusement quite indescribable. His district included several counties and everywhere he went a crowd filled all the available space in the court room, staying there as long as court remained in session.

His remarks caused a continuous merriment that he made no effort to suppress. His utterances passed from mouth to mouth through the country, and to this day constitute a part of the folklore of the localities where he presided. I do not know of his ever quoting any bit of humor from any source or that he ever repeated himself. All appeared spontaneous and was the most mirth-provoking when he appeared to be most in earnest. He had some legal knowledge, but his decisions were guided mostly by an intuitive perception of human nature.

His judgments were seldom reversed. The public suffered most by the increased expense which his peculiar conduct caused, and the delay that necessarily accompanied such a practice. I will narrate a few incidents of his career, protesting that without the setting it is difficult to give a clear idea of the effect produced.

Here is a description of his homely method in sentencing a convict. The judge scratched his head and ran his fingers through his hair for several minutes as if in very deep meditation, then turning to the prisoner at the bar said: "You've been convicted of keeping a disorderly house. It's my duty to punish you. Now, I'll never know whether I have given you enough or not, but I have got to guess at it."

Then, hesitating a moment and scratching his head again, he continued: "If you were some old woman, toothless and destitute, Children crying for bread, and was trying to keep the wolf from the door, there might have been some mitigating circumstances. But there you are, a great strong man, able to earn an honest living, and think of you keeping a place for dis reputable people to congregate and aggregate, and for men and boys to hang around and sit around. Ain't you ashamed of yourself? When I think of it my blood boils and I feel like retiring you to the cemetery. Then the better angel of my nature asserts itself and I can't help but pity such a miserable cuss as you are!"

With this the judge began to catch for breath, and his eyes filled with tears. Putting his hands over his face, he blubbered: "I tell you, judges have feelings same as other folks."

Then his tone changed, and he swelled with wrath as he descanted upon the enormity of the offense and its effect upon the public, saying: "Such crimes breed other crimes, just as mice breed mice." All who witnessed this violent tirade against the prisoner expected that the judge would give him the limit. The prisoner looked crestfallen and wilted like the frost-nipped pump kin vine.

Finally, the judge wound up by fining him fifty dollars and costs. His leaning toward the side of mercy made him a "habeas corpus" judge. In these proceedings many bound over to the grand jury sought release on the ground that the evidence was not enough to hold them. A man so held for cattle stealing produced the one who had stolen the cattle to testify that the prisoner had no knowledge of it, and the feelings of his neighbors were so very strong in his favor that while the argument was in progress wealthy friends shouted, "He isn't guilty! Everybody knows he isn't guilty. We will go his bond for any amount," etc.

This was designed to influence the court to discharge him. But in rendering his decision the judge said: "If this man was unable to give a bond and would be dragged from his family to jail and lie there until the grand jury comes to town, I would discharge him, for I do not believe there is evidence enough to convict him, but here are a lot of good, respectable citizens who are anxious to go his bond, and I think I ought to let them do it just for luck." And so he was held to the grand jury.

In another case of a similar nature a woman had been bound over for stealing a wisp of hair, and it appeared from the evidence that she had previously borne a good reputation. In discharging her the judge seemed deeply affected. He enlarged upon the evidence of her good character and of the long years that she had denied herself the pleasures of life to acquire it, and now it was proposed to take this priceless thing from her for a wisp of hair. He said it would take just thirteen men to perform such an outrage. Then, increasing in vehement emotion, he exclaimed: "If I were one of the jury before I'd bring in such a verdict I'd hang! I'd hang till the ants carried me out of the keyhole. I'd hang till the great white angel would stand with one foot on the sea and the other on the land and swear that time shall be no more!"

On the Fourth of July an old man was arrested for drunkenness and placed in a village calaboose. Two young men in the presence of multitude had broken open the receptacle and taken him out. They were bound over for aiding a prisoner to escape. In hearing on habeas corpus the judge discharged the young men on the ground that they had not aided the prisoner to escape because the evidence showed that he was so drunk that he was not trying to escape. In his opinion the judge said: "If the recording angel had looked down and witnessed the sufferings of this poor old man, confined within those slimy walls, and the efforts of these brave boys to relieve him, he would have dropped a tear and blotted the record out."

A suit relative to a savings bank that had suspended payment brought out the following: "These savings banks remind me of the alligators I used to know when I was a boy. They would smear their under jaws with sweet weeds and lie along the riverside as if they were dead, with their mouths wide open. The flies and bugs and insects would roost on their under jaws. Sometimes a toad or frog would hop up there to get in the shade. When the under jaw was well covered down would come the upper jaw." The savings bank had suspended.

A banker who owned a farm testified in a case that he was a farmer. Speaking of this witness, Judge Wind said: "There's two kinds of farmers: those who farm the farms and those who farm the farmers. Those who get up in the morning when the big red sun is just peeking over the horizon and go out and slop the pigs, water the horses and do all the chores before breakfast. After breakfast they go out and work hard all day on the farm and get callouses all over their hands. They are what I call the horny-handed farmers. Then there are those who sit behind mahogany counters and have a chronometer safe and watch the clock for their rent and interest to fall due. They are what I call the horny-seated farmers. And this wit ness is that kind."

Sometimes his metaphors were not appropriate. Once while describing a battle he was telling of the awful tumult made by the artillery, when he said: "The thunder of the mighty guns rose peal on peal like an onion." Nor was he always exact in his dates. On one occasion he said: "Fourteen hundred and ninety-two years ago to-day Columbus discovered America." The clerk of his court pulled his sleeve and said: "Judge, you mean in the year 1492." "I repeat," continued the judge in a still louder tone, "fourteen hundred and ninety-two years ago Colum bus discovered America." His clerk again jerked his sleeve and tried to correct him, but, raising his voice still louder, the judge ex claimed: "As I said before, 1492 years ago Christopher Columbus discovered America, there or thereabouts."

When attempting to describe the state of his mind on a certain subject, he said: "I feel like a fellow who has just moved into a store and has his goods scattered all around, topsy-turvy, some on the floor, some in boxes, some on the counters. I've got a full stock of knowledge on this subject, but I haven't got it sorted out and put away on the shelves. I don't assume to know everything. Because some fellow differs from me I don't say he knows less than I do. I don't put up any Procrustean bed to compel everybody to lie on. Because a man is longer than I am I don't want to cut him off. If he is shorter I don't want to hammer him out. I am willing to hear everything everybody has to say and guess at it, then if they don't like it there is a lot of fellows over there at the capital who can try their hands at guessing. What we don't any of us know would make mighty big book."

The foregoing shows the characteristics of this judge. A full account of his career would contain great number of similar ebullitions. All afforded much amusement. The judge did not belong to the dominant party which had a majority of many thousands in his district; yet he was re-elected for many years without effort. The people complained of court expenses, delays in trials, the leniency of the judge, the lightness of his sentences, the escape of rascals on habeas corpus, but when the time came to vote they forgot their grievances and gave their suffrages for the quaint old judge who had so frequently amused them.

Sometimes a little dash of humor may relieve the monotony of court proceedings and do no great harm. But its indulgence by the judge encourages similar efforts by others. The practice grows until the business of the court is sidetracked by numerous efforts of the judge and attorneys to be amusing. The better practice is for the judge to concentrate his attention upon the subject in hand and try to attract the attention of all others to the same subject. The business is serious and should not be made the occasion for frivolity. The man whose life, liberty or property are at stake and sees his rights made the subject of merriment will never be able to appreciate the jokes. This disposition for display should be curbed. The judge bothered with surplus energy in this direction should bottle it up and not pull the cork until he leaves the bench.

CHAPTER VIII.

Corruption.

All will admit the most important element of judicial character is honesty. If the judge has all the other qualifications and lacks this he cannot be considered a good judge. If he has this he may lack others and yet be endured and for given. Corruption in a judge is a crime that can never be condoned.

The members of the City Council may sell the birthright of posterity for many generations and cram their pockets to overflowing. We endure it. The mayor may unite with blacklegs and draw rich profits from illegal enterprises. We hold our noses and vote for his re-election. Legislators may become the truckling tools of corporate greed and cover the statutes with stealing machines to fleece us of our savings.

They may elect their family domestics committee clerks and stuff the payrolls of the state with the names of their "sisters, their cousins and their aunts." We bear that, too. The Congress of the United States may be the sanctuary of thieves and the headquarters for all forms of rascality. Our patience still abides. The national Senate may become the paid agents of plunderers and form a conspiracy against justice and human rights. We grit our teeth and do not explode. Even the President of the United States might turn his back upon the people who elected him and use his vast power to enrich himself and his family and impoverish us. He may treat his official oath and the Constitution of the United States as useless forms.

We still keep our hands in our pockets, grip what we have got, trust in God and hope for the millennium. But when we have a case in court and ascertain to a certainty that the judge is bribed to decide against us, even if the case involves only the worth of a bag of peanuts, we feel a thirst for revenge that nothing can assuage. We may be so tender-hearted that we would step out of the ordinary path to avoid crushing the angleworm that fell in the shower.

We may be so kind to wards all animate nature that we would rather live upon vegetables than kill any animal, bird or fish. But when we think of the act of this judge, he appears so damnably mean that we wish we could see him hamstrung and fed to the buzzards. We would like to have him nailed to the cross of torture and drive the nails ourselves and could enjoy his groans of agony as if they were heavenly music. No punishment would be too great to glut our vengeance. Even the rascals who do the dirty job despise the judge who has yielded to them.

The fear that a judge may be corrupt paralyzes the efforts of the lawyer and deprives him of all courage to try the case. He feels as if he had been gagged by the emissaries of iniquity and become utterly helpless in their hands. There are probably-many more judges suspected of corruption than are guilty, but comparatively few of those guilty are discovered. So sly are the underground methods used to reach the occupants of the bench that they come to light only when they are uncovered by accident. I wish now to turn a searchlight upon the machine which forms and finishes the corrupt judge. I wish to exhibit its spindles, cogs, drive-wheels, belts, line shafting, pulleys and the hands that manipulate it. For this purpose, I will present Judge Graft for your consideration.

Judge Graft.

He was the darling of well-to-do and fond parents, who reared him in love and luxury and gave him a good education in the best college. He was unusually bright by nature, had a fine form, a handsome face, a sparkling eye, and a scintillating wit. His smile was winning. He was at once recognized as a good fellow everywhere. He was capable of preparing himself for any position which man can fill. This is how he was fashioned into a corrupt judge.

He looked about him in the world and he heard many voices glorifying riches. Thousands of these came to him from out the past singing the praises of the wealthy and powerful. Myriads of bells all over the land chimed te-deums to those who had grabbed and gathered the greatest quantity of earth's substance. He went to church and the perfumed pastor standing behind banks of flowers hung wreaths of roses about the names of rich men. In the newspapers and magazines he read long columns describing the glittering flummery of the millionaire's family. He saw whirl by him on the street the splendid automobile of the renowned doctor who had won the favor and patronage of the wealthy. He listened to the panegyrics that were delivered over the corpse of the old lawyer who had expired in the service of a great corporate monopoly.

On the other hand, he saw honest poverty shivering in the shadows of palaces, begging for a place to toil, eating the crusts that it had earned in the sight of the contemptuous rich. He concluded he must have wealth, and he nerved every fiber of his being to the task. The old way of earning more and spending less seemed too slow for him. He wanted to get money without giving an equivalent. He hoped that fortune would shower upon him wealth that he had not earned. He acquired that passion for gambling which flourishes in every land under the sun. He played the races. He hung about bucket-shops and watched the ticker. He entered eagerly into all kinds of gambling games.

As a lawyer he neglected his books. He courted the society of the rich, and he toadied at the feet of the powerful. He contracted expenses beyond his means. He married a girl who had never earned a dollar nor wished to save a cent. Her mind was full of frivolity and she wanted to load her limbs with the costliest jewels and fabrics. She picked his pockets for his last dollar and made his days and nights hideous with her clamors for more. They had children, each of whom became a greater expense than an ordinary family.

His earnings were large, but his expenses were larger. His habits were convivial. He strained himself constantly to keep afloat in fashionable society. Soon he was swamped with indebtedness, and when placed on the bench needed money as a drowning man needs air. He was in a whirl pool of financial difficulties, out of which he could not swim. His situation was so desperate that had a devil thrown him a line he would have grabbed it gladly.

As judge he had millions passing through his hands. Fortunes were handed from one to another in accordance with his decisions. A slight deviation from the law and the facts made or unmade a millionaire. Now, suppose that some suitor told this judge's wife if a case before her husband was decided a certain way she would be presented with the mortgage on the homestead, or that one of her children would be given a Christmas present of a block of stock the value of which depended on the decision its father might make, would such a man so situated be likely to indulge in paroxysms of rage? Would he not defend himself by saying: "This was the way I intended to decide the case. This money which I so much need is a benefaction of Fortune."

Could he not invent many excuses which would seem justifiable and permit him to receive indirectly the bribe intended to corrupt him? This once accepted, he is no longer a free man. His secret is in the hands of scoundrels. Ever afterwards it is simply a question of price. He started on the road to depravity when his mind first indulged the idea of getting wealth without earning it. This is one way of making a corrupt judge. There are many others. Often the lawyer serves a term as a bribe-giver or lobbyist before being elevated to the bench. In such cases the transition is not so sharp. If a lawyer has habitually hired himself out to advocate false pleas, put forward sham defenses and other subterfuges for delay and to wear out the plaint if for to enable the guilty to escape, if he has become the tool of criminals, either corporations or individuals, who are constantly violating or evading the law, when he is elected to the bench he has hardly character enough to be worth buying or courage enough to resist those who would control his decisions. He is considered bought. He gets bribes only by begging for them.

There are many degrees of honesty. Some are so scrupulously just that they prefer to give to everyone his due. Others will be honest to a neighbor or friend but will not hesitate to cheat a stranger or an enemy. Those who would beat a railroad company out of passenger fare or swindle the general government by false claims for mileage could not be induced to accept a bribe or cheat a landlord out of his hotel bill.

Men who would forge or steal a pass or ticket into a theater would quickly return a pocketbook which they found upon the street. Dishonesty is a kind of habit which grows upon people out of the environment in which they are placed, and like all bad habits it begins with the small variety and goes from bad to worse. If one would be impervious to temptation he must be honest everywhere and at all times; he must not desire to receive from any source anything for which he has not paid or intends to pay a just equivalent.

All passes, free tickets and gifts intended to win favor are calculated to debauch both the giver and receiver. The complicated machinery of our government should have men to operate it who propose to be absolutely just, and candidates for judicial positions should be men of this character who live within their means, pay their debts promptly and are neither beggars nor receivers of gifts and favors from anyone likely to have business before their courts. When the lawyer has become a judge he should at once divorce himself from all alliances that are likely to influence his decisions. When the coquette of the village wins the prize she has sought and becomes a married lady she will, if she is wise, change her conduct and demean herself so as to retain the confidence of her husband.

And the lawyer when he is elevated to the bench should immediately cease flirting with corporations and refuse all special favors offered him because of his position. If he does this he will soon be marked as an irreproachable. He will be blacklisted on the roll kept by bribe-givers and he will have thereafter no temptations to resist. It is not enough for the judge to be honest in fact; he should so conduct himself as to convince the world of his integrity and give no ground for suspicion if he is to reach the highest success. Honesty and fairness must be written upon the face of everything he does and appear in every emanation from his mind and every joint and motion of his body.

CHAPTER IX.

Pugnacity.

There is in most natures something that rebels against dictation, that refuses to believe without proof, and squares itself to maintain its ground, resisting all efforts at dislodgment. This quality is the basis of conservatism. It is a kind of spinal column to the thought structure of the race. If developed to an excessive degree it blockades the path of progress and degenerates into a senseless opposition which loves contest for contest's sake. One of its manifestations is that spirit of criticism, everywhere rife, which delights in tearing down idols, collecting and magnifying defects, and striving to give the impression that there is really nothing in the world worthwhile except the finding of fault. Occasionally this spirit gets on the bench and becomes a serious obstruction in the administration of justice.

Judge Whiffet.

Judge Whiffet was the only son of extraordinary parents. His father was a champion heavy weight pugilist. His mother was tall, angular and powerful, both mentally and physically. She headed every movement in the community for the emancipation of her sex, socially, religiously, and politically. The solitary offspring of this remarkable pair was such a weazen, shriveled little imp that few thought he could survive and grow to manhood.

The current of his life had evidently started in a drouth, for after he had ceased growing he was still undersize and had the appearance of being poorly nourished except in his hair and beard. These were unusually luxuriant and were cultivated with great care, so that his head and face were as full blown as a hairy chrysanthemum, in which were small holes for two little pale blue eyes and a pinched pug nose. The ladies said he was a darling, but the male species were less kind. Some declared he was a poodle, others a baboon. From infancy he was a tireless objector and an irrepressible dissenter. He evidently became dissatisfied at an early age with the form in which nature had fashioned him, and he began at once to kick. What he lacked in physical strength he made up in mental opposition. His chief delight was to pull down and drag out the pets of people.

He took pleasure in claiming their money to be counterfeit, their gods devils, what they supposed to be virtue vice, and what they admired as beauty the quintessence of ugliness. His thin voice was jerky and very rapid in its utterance. He stopped at intervals to spit. He could speak about three hundred words a minute and spit about fifty times in doing so. He rarely spoke except to contradict, and usually began with "No, no, no, tut, tut, tut," beating the circumambient air a rat-tat-too with his "Tut, tut, tut," speaking so rapidly and with such audacious assurance that no one cared to undertake the hopeless task of interrupting him. When a lad he attended every gathering where there was a chance of starting an argument.

Even in Sunday school and church he managed to stir up a great commotion and get everybody out of the proper reverential calm and into a ferment. Political meetings were his favorite haunts, and there from an obscure place in the audience he would launch questions at the speaker and thus turn the meeting into a fierce discussion or cause it to break up in arrow.

While at college his favorite sport was the debating societies. There he was a terror. Sometimes when he had opened a discussion on a subject and none could be found to take the opposite side, he would take that side himself and make as earnest an argument in opposition to his first position as he had before made in favor of it. This spirit of controversy grew on him until it became a veritable disease.

As soon as a proposition was asserted his mind immediately took the other side and became filled with arguments to the contrary. At the table, if anyone found fault with an article of diet, he at once began to eat of it eagerly, declaring that it was the best he had ever tasted. At a dance he always chose the wall-flowers as partners. He was sure the majority were always wrong, the worst thieves were in office and the best citizens in the penitentiary. This trait made him quite popular.

Many grow weary of public dolls and enjoy seeing them lacerated and shown to be stuffed with sawdust. The man who argues that every plank in the ship of state is worm-eaten will never lack an applauding audience. Who makes it plain that the management of the universe is unreliable and that everything is on the toboggan slide to destruction will ever gather about him a large crowd who will pound their extremities in gleeful approval.

The bold and dashing courage which Whiffet often exhibited in pitting his personal views against a multitude of opponents was admired even by those who had no sympathy with them. On one occasion he attended a meeting of prohibitionists. Many strong addresses were delivered denouncing intoxicants. The sentiment seemed unanimous against the traffic, when Mr. Whiffet popped up, exclaiming, "No, no, no, tut, tut, tut! I know all about it. I have swallowed enough liquor to float a steamboat. The Esquimaux takes it to get warm. The Hottentot drinks it to get cool. You can't mix a medicine, pickle a snake or raise a barn without it! You pale, mush-and-milk prohibitionists haven't blood enough in your veins to stain waste paper! I was brought up on the bottle and take naturally to the jug. A little corn juice would start your livers and give your blue noses a touch of sun set!"

Thus he continued, ridiculing and assailing them until the meeting collapsed. At a Fourth of July celebration he startled everybody by taking the stand after the oration was finished and attempted to defend George the Third. He also tried to prove that Washington was a grafter, who located the national capital on his farm; that Ben Franklin was a masher, and that Thomas Jefferson was a slaveholder. Perhaps the most peculiar instance of Judge Whiffet's opposition was the occasion when a Sunday evening meeting was held in one of the largest churches, to protest against what was termed the "pictures of naked Women" posted on the billboards about the city.

After many speeches were made denouncing these pictures Judge Whiffet bounded into the arena with his "No, no, no, tut, tut, tut!" rattling through the auditorium. All eyes were focused upon him. "I know all about this matter !" he ex claimed. "These pictures don't look like anybody. Who is soft enough to fall in love with a bill board picture? Look at the old man on the front page of the almanac! Why don't you preachers make him put on his clothes? See the saints and angels in your illustrated bibles in their night shirts! If you people are so weak-minded that you can't look upon a billboard picture without feeling sinful sensations, you had better put a mother-hub bard on the Goddess of Liberty, and catch old Father Time with his scythe and give him a pair of pantaloons!" Thus he continued for three-quarters of an hour and kept the whole audience convulsed with laughter. The management forgot their resolutions, neglected to take up the collection, and went to their several homes grinning at the ridiculous termination of the meeting.

At the bar he was usually attorney for the defendant. He always claimed the state was persecuting the innocent, that the police and state's attorney were in conspiracy to rob a saint of liberty or life. Persons suing for personal injuries he always considered were putting up a job on the defendant, usually a guileless corporation, hoping by feigning injuries and perjuring themselves to get dishonest money. On the bench he exhibited the same spirit of controversy. He opposed every assertion. He interrupted lawyers in argument and plied them with questions which scattered their thoughts and filled their minds with confusion.

None thus pestered could properly present their views. Often he pounced upon witnesses and tried to argue them out of their recollections. By this strenuous op position he made all who attempted to give him any information feel that they were discredited and that he was determined to thwart their

*efforts. This seriously impaired the sources of his infor-
mation and made it impossible for anyone to fully present a
case for his consideration.*

*But even worse than this was its effect upon the judgment of
the judge himself. To be impartial a judge must avoid forming an opinion before a full hearing is had. If he allows his
mind to entertain a notion sufficiently strong to start a discussion, he thereby contracts a bias that re quires force to
dislodge.*

*His efforts to defend his position make the bias still stronger
and put a further obstruction in the way of an impartial decision. Judges of the highest courts certainly do not realize
this when they start arguments with the lawyers who are discussing questions before them. There may be cases where it
is proper for a judge to interrupt counsel and ask him a question, but the judge should wait until the counsel has finished
on the point under discussion, and when the question is answered the judge should subside without comment or any expression indicating pleasure or displeasure.*

The spirit of controversy should abide only with attorneys. The judge ought to watch the contest entirely un-
affected with the fervor. By pitching into the discussion he exposes his unfitness, creates confusion and
impairs the confidence of one or both parties. Men so
tainted with an appetite for controversy that they cannot control it should realize that they are not adapted

to the bench. They should remain at the bar or seek legislative or other offices where they can indulge their favorite sport.

CHAPTER X.

Additional Varieties.

The judges sketched in the foregoing pages are leading types, but there are many variations and combinations of these types, to which I can make but slight reference, lest I weary the reader.

There is the tippling judge, who derives his judicial inspiration from spirituous liquors. One should not be surprised at any treatment from him. I once tried a chancery suit before such a judge for several days. Much evidence was taken in support of the bill and crossbill. When the attorneys on each side appeared to argue the case, each claiming prior equity to the property in controversy, the judge came upon the bench so maudlin drunk that his thick tongue made his words difficult of utterance. He refused to hear any argument, and without giving any reason whatever ordered the bill and cross-bill dis missed, and the clerk entered the order. A drunkard in possession of the scales of justice is a most disgusting sight.

I know of another case where the judge and both attorneys were hilarious with liquor. The judge interrupted one of the attorneys in his argument and said: "Sit down, Dan; you can't stuff sod corn down the neck of this court." This enraged the attorney, who grabbed the judge by the coat collar, jerked him from the bench to the floor and began pounding him on the back of the neck with his fist. The sheriff interfered, exclaiming: "Dan, what are you doing?" Dan replied: "The cuss has ruled against me and I am taking my exceptions!" At one time it was very common for lawyers and judges to be more or less intoxicated when engaged in the discharge of their functions, but I think it will now be con ceded that the drunkard is not fit for the bench. The judicial mind should be unclouded from any such a source.

Then there is the sociable judge, who makes a special effort to be familiar with the parties, their attorneys, and the witnesses. I once tried a case involving more than a million dollars before a judge, and during the intervals of the adjournments the judge and my opponent usually dined and went bicycle riding together. I had another case where a young lady was trying to establish an interest in an estate, and after the case was tried and taken under advisement, the judge visted the lady at her room and made several attempts at undue familiarity. The sociable judge is ready at all times to talk about the case with either party or his attorney, whether the op posing counsel is present or otherwise. He will introduce the subject himself, call you into his chambers or stand on the street corner or lounge about the hotel and discuss the questions so freely as to cause you a deal of uneasiness. In doing this he may not intend any wrong, but the impression made is very unfavorable and greatly impairs the confidence of the side which is not successful.

There is also the gaming judge, who spends much of his hours when off the bench in games of chance, and devotes more attention in watching the accidental combination of cards than in considering treatises on law or the decisions of the courts. The writer once argued a motion to amend the findings of fact made by an Appellate Court in a case involving over ninety thousand dollars, when the judges hearing the argument were engaged in playing cards, and they managed it with such adroitness as not to allow the argument to interrupt the game. It cost my client more than one thousand dollars to correct the error which they then made. Judges must have some recreation and

amusement, and if the trial of a lawsuit is not a sufficient game of chance, then they can indulge the spirit
of gam bling by playing the races, rattling poker chips,
and whirling the wheel of fortune, but this passion
ought not to become so furious that they cannot stop
the game long enough to attend to their judicial duties.
Many a time has court adjourned for the judge to attend a horse race or ballgame. A large proportion of
the adjournments from Saturday over to Tuesday are
for the purpose of giving the judge an opportunity to
indulge his favorite passion.

There is the invalid judge, who spends his winters in
Florida and his summers in Alaska, migrating with the
wild geese, and is rarely on the bench long enough to
try a protracted suit or do anything of importance except draw his breath and his salary. Every lawyer has
suffered at his hands and yet dislikes to complain because of sympathy for his affliction.

The moss-grown docket of this judge acts as a sinkhole
or catch-basin into which controversies are thrown,
there to remain undecided until the patience or life of
the suitors is exhausted. The longevity of these inva-
lids is most remarkable and can only be equaled by the
patient endurance of the foolish public who re-elect
them after their terms expire. They will live to take
castor oil, Turkish baths and various forms of patent

medicines until long after we are gathered to our fathers.

May God preserve their lives and, in his mercy, remove them from the bench.

The vacation judge may next be noticed. He is always overworked and about to start on a vacation. With the slightest excuse or with no excuse at all, he adjourns his court so frequently, and is on the bench so short a time on any one occasion that he does but little business. As soon as you have discovered that he is sitting and have arranged to have your case brought up before him, you learn he is about to take another trip, either to Europe, Asia or Africa, to recuperate his overworked and exhausted energies.

The vacation judge abounds principally in the large cities, and if he were employed by private parties it would soon be discovered that he did not earn his salary and he would be dismissed. The public, however, does not murmur and the lawyers and their clients submit gracefully, and the life of the vacation judge becomes one long picnic at the general expense. Such a judge is a barnacle upon our system of jurisprudence. His uncertain and indolent habits become contagious, not only among the members of the bench, but of the bar. If judges were paid for the time they actually hold court this evil would disappear.

Another variety is what I will call the chambers judge. A large part of the time which he should employ on the bench is taken up in his private room, wherein he sees visitors, keeping attorneys, suitors, and witnesses waiting for him to appear, while he carries on private interviews with lawyers, politicians, and personal friends. This practice is sometimes indulged in until it becomes a great source of annoyance to litigants, seriously impairs the efficiency of the judge, and deprives the public of the benefit of a large part of his services. Strictly speaking, the judge has no more right to keep others waiting than they have to keep him waiting. He is a public servant and he should be promptly on the bench at the time appointed, prepared to do the work for which he is paid.

The written opinion judge is another kind. He feels called upon to give the reasons in writing for many of his decisions and puts off the announcements of them until he can write these reasons, and when they are written, instead of filing the writing for such persons to read as may desire, he insists upon keeping a large crowd of people waiting while he slowly and wearily reads his long-drawn-out production, of no interest to anyone except the attorneys in the particular case. Such judges used to be common on the Supreme benches of the country, but now they are mostly found in the lower courts. In a community where nearly everyone can read, and where the production does not depend upon elocutionary skill for its effect, no reason can be given for thus wasting the valuable time of the public. The written opinion judge should take a hint and desist.

Another species is the compromise judge, who thinks that every case ought to be in some way compromised and spends much of his time in an effort to induce the parties to settle and agree upon the amount of the judgment. He uses his power and makes many erroneous rulings, hoping thereby to intimidate the stubborn suitor into adopting his suggestions, and if he fails in this and there is a verdict for the plaintiff, he usually forces him to accept a reduction to prevent the granting of a new trial. Thus the judge abdicates the role of a jurist for that of a peacemaker and meddles where he has no right, and thus prevents the attainment of legal justice. The parties must themselves determine whether they will settle or have a trial and the judge should keep his hands off, except where he is called upon to render a decision.

Then there is the technical judge, who wastes the time of the public in mooting and discussing trivial distinctions and tissue paper partitions of no consequence to the merits of the case, as if looking for some way to prevent deciding the real controversy. By various windings, twisting's, and quibbling's, many of which he conjures up unsolicited by either side, this judge makes a lawsuit appear mysterious to the ignorant and farcical to the intelligent. His mental gymnastics are too expensive. He should spend his time on the merits of the case.

Another is the story telling variety, the judge who at each stage of the proceeding is reminded of a story supposed to possess more or less point or humor. The crowd in waiting cannot escape and are forced to listen, and must pretend to be interested in the tale, to laugh where it is intended to be funny, and exhibit such other emotions as the judge is trying to inspire. None dares refuse to laugh at the judge's joke or fail to appreciate the point in his narration. A judge can in this way waste time of more value than the amount of his salary. He should be jarred hard enough to awaken his sense of propriety.

Another peculiar species is the contempt judge, who often finds it necessary to punish lawyers, parties, witnesses, and bystanders for showing disrespect to his person or his authority. These contempt proceedings squander a large part of the time which belongs to the public. The judge rarely secures for himself the respect of which he thinks he has been deprived, and because of these proceedings he is usually held in greater contempt by more people than he would have been had he not resorted to them, a judge whose conduct naturally inspires disrespect can no more make himself respected by contempt proceedings than an acrobat can lift himself by his boot-straps.

The nepotic judge is another. He uses his power to get offices for his relatives as bailiffs, receivers, masters in chancery, putting persons without merit in these places. This judge is usually a grafter and has many other ways of diverting the public funds into his own pocket. The abuse of official power in this manner by officers in other branches of the government may be tolerated, but in the judicial it is too rank and must be extirpated, root and branch.

The aspiring judge may next claim attention. He is a perennial candidate for offices of all kinds. He has hardly warmed his seat on the bench when he begins scheming for several other positions and to this end uses all the public machinery over which he has control. Much of his time is consumed in attending political meetings, caucuses and conventions and in consorting with professional politicians, ward heelers and strikers. His mind is filled with visions of preferment for himself and with plans to assist his understrappers. The mental pabulum that he should consume in the public service is exhausted in these extraneous pursuits, and it is difficult for suitors to believe that he is capable of giving them an unbiased judgment.

This judge must be curbed. Would it not be well for the law to make a judge ineligible for any other office during the term for which he is elected, and forbid under penalty of forfeiting his judicial position the seeking by him of any other office?

Then there is the notoriety-seeking judge, who is always rendering some remarkable or sensational decision, and who keeps a squad of newspaper reporters about him and sometimes has a press agent to fill the newspapers with his doings. He constantly strives to occupy the center of the stage, where the spot light is the brightest, and spends much time in self-conscious posing and parade. These distracting influences impair the quality of his decisions and diminish the quantity of the work that he performs and causes him to lose the esteem of members of the legal profession and of his associates on the bench.

The procrastinating judge is a great source of vexation to parties and their attorneys. He takes motions, demurrers, and submitted cases under advisement and puts off the decisions until he forgets all about them. Finally attorneys weary of waiting call them to his attention. Then the matters must be again argued or he renders a decision which is a mere guess, based upon his indistinct recollection. In this way suits are caused to drag for years, the parties deprived of redress and the law's delay becomes a proverbial grievance. There seems no way of preventing this practice except the enactment of a statute requiring a judge to render a decision within a reasonable time. Ten days ought to be long enough to consider and decide that which has been fully argued and submitted.

The scolding judge is another kind and is a most disagreeable nuisance. He keeps everybody before him stirred up with his fault-finding and complaining and makes life in and about his court-room most unpleasant. Our ancestors punished the woman who became a common scold with the ducking stool, by which she was three times publicly ducked. This certainly was a mild chastisement. If a nervous, broken-down, ignorant old woman ought to be ducked for scolding, a strong, healthy, educated man, who has been placed upon the bench, ought to be drowned for the same offense.

The toadying judge is often seen. The practicing lawyer will occasionally meet on the bench a judge who takes delight in showing unusual courtesy toward renowned persons. When a prominent lawyer from another locality, or one who occupies a leading position at the bar appears before him, this judge is unduly affected and makes an unseemly spectacle of himself in his efforts to show consideration for this lawyer. Likewise when a noted man appears either as a party or a witness, the judge does so much bowing and scraping as to attract general attention. This causes onlookers and especially the jury to infer that the person so peculiarly honored is believed by the judge to be a superior being and what he says is of unusual weight and credit. Such toadyism is a species of partiality very unbecoming in the occupant of the bench. In this country where all are equal before the law, he should treat all people, from the proudest to the humblest, from the most famous to the least known, with exactly the same courtesy and consideration. He brands himself a sycophant when he toadys to anybody.

The sympathetic judge is also often found on the bench. He melts quickly at the sight of distress and is moved to pity by tales of sorrow and need. Lawyers who have been much engaged in defending persons charged with crime and in prosecuting cases for personal injuries are often so tender hearted that they cannot be relied upon to decide questions of law and evidence fairly and impartially when one of the parties to the suit is poor, weak or sorely afflicted.

The jury are notorious in their bias in favor of the weak against the strong, the individual against the corporation, the woman against the man, and when to their bias is added the bias of the judge along the same line the loses its balance, throws away its scales, and is stampeded to the rescue of the parties in distress. The lawyer who cannot look upon misery and maintain his balance, whose eyes are likely to be blinded with tears at a spectacle of suffering, should never aspire to the bench. His place is at the bar, or in some charitable work where he can incite people to relieve suffering. On the bench he is likely to pick the pockets of the rich to bestow charity upon the poor.

The corporation judge should not be missed. His principal employment at the bar has been in defending corporations and his experience has lead him to believe they cannot get a fair trial before a jury, especially in personal injury cases. To prevent the property of these institutions from being confiscated by unjust verdicts he thinks it his duty to strain every point in their favor in such cases. Accordingly he makes the path of the plaintiff's attorney as difficult and uncomfortable as possible.

He denies to him the same opportunity to produce evidence and enforces stricter rules in its ad mission. He examines with a microscope the instructions asked on behalf of the plaintiff and often takes the case from the jury and orders the verdict for the defendant where the evidence is conflicting and the plaintiff is entitled to have a jury pass upon the case. That some provocation exists for such prejudice all must admit, but no judge should consider the corporations of the country as his wards. The judge is not required to pass upon the wisdom of the law that provides for a jury trial, by substituting his own ideas of what is right for the verdict of the jury, fie should enforce the law as it is leaving the consequences to the legislature. This is difficult for one who has for many years been employed in defending such suits. "What's bred in the bone will come out in the marrow."

This branch of litigation has greatly increased especially in cities where it composes fully one half of the litigated cases and it may be doubted, whether the public who should be careful to elect unbiased judges, ought to place upon the bench those whose previous experiences have created such a marked bias in favor of their former clients. Sometimes these corporation lawyers realize that they are biased and in their efforts to guard against it may go to the other extreme. This is quite as bad.

I will here bring this chapter to a close, realizing that I have omitted to introduce many specimens which probably deserve attention as much as any noticed. All tend in one way or another to increase the cost of court proceedings and impair the quality of work done. Judges like other men must be expected to have their foibles and it is hoped that calling public attention to them in a good-natured way will awaken a desire for improvement, thereby greatly benefiting the public as well as the legal profession.

CHAPTER XI.

Abuses.

It has ever been the tendency of power to beget abuses. Every department of government is likely to become their nesting place. The judicial branch is no exception. The emanation from the judge is only his opinion and usually on a subject where there is such latitude for difference that no conclusion need impugn his integrity. Hence, he may favor friends and relatives, advance certain pet theories or measures, curry favor with powerful interests or follow his own sympathies, and his motives not be questioned.

The judges sometimes yield to temptation and that judicial power is frequently abused is the belief of every lawyer, and yet, if any were asked to prove specific instances, he would experience great difficulty. There have, however, from time to time, grown up and become common, certain practices which are more prevalent name for them than to call them abuses. I am aware that in referring to them I run the risk of offending some who are profiting by the practices, but I beg such to consider that the subject is an unpleasant one to me and one I would gladly avoid.

I do not blame the beneficiaries of these abuses, for most persons placed in the same situation would do likewise. I also hesitate to criticize the members of the bench, for I have no doubt this body of men taken together are of the most worthy in our country and are entitled to the highest commendation for their learning, integrity and industry. But higher than the Supreme Court, greater than the Republic, and of more sublime worth than any human character are the great principles of Truth and Justice.

There is no pedestal so lofty that its occupant must not prostrate himself before these principles. As long as there is an intelligent management of the Universe these will rule the hearts and consciences of men, and force multitudes into the arena to fight for their maintenance. Courts may call themselves supreme and in the plentitude of their power gloat upon the conclusion that their decisions can never be reversed. Let such be not deceived, for at that moment when official power becomes most arrogant it totters to its fall.

There is a limit beyond which the governed will not endure abuses, and like the slumbering volcano which explodes from the silent summit, or the tornado which gathers in the quiet air, popular discontent may accumulate until it bursts forth and hurls from their seats all those who in their imagined security have betrayed their trusts and lay in one common ruin all the criminal forces that have connived at the betrayal. No official is so high that he can afford to escape criticism or be deaf to the murmurs of discontent. Therefore, out of kindness to the occupants of the bench I offer a few suggestions which I trust will be welcome to all those who are fit to occupy such positions.

The road to the fountain of justice should be short and straight and not blockaded with so many toll-gates that no one can enter her temple without paving his way with gold. The poor have greater need to seek redress in the courts than the rich and they must not be excluded therefrom on account of their poverty. Good citizens must therefore view with anxious concern all devices calculated to increase court expenses. The body of our jurisprudence has accumulated a lot of expensive leaches which ought to be dislodged.

THE PRINTING ABUSE.

Before the typewriter came into general use the practice was adopted of requiring abstracts of record, briefs and arguments for the Appellate and Supreme

Courts to be printed in a certain size type so as to make a specified form of printed document. This was supposed to facilitate the reading of such papers by the judges. When the practice was first introduced, records were small, briefs were short and the expense light, but through the aid of the shorthand reporter and the vast accumulation of authorities, this printing bill has now become prodigious, and the burden laid upon the litigants intolerable.

The typewriter is capable of making four copies with one impression that are good enough for anyone to read and if there ever was a reason for this printing expense to accommodate the judges it has passed away. I think it may be fairly estimated that the cost to litigants alone caused by this practice is more than the amount of the salaries paid to the judges thus accommodated. So great is this that poor suitors are often denied the right of a review of their cases because they are unable to pay it.

THE REFERENCE ABUSE.

Courts of Chancery have long exercised the right to refer certain cases to an appointee called a Master, and it is not doubted but that some matters have arisen where such a reference facilitates the administration of Justice. But the practice has grown until now nearly all contested chancery suits and even default cases are so referred. The formality and expense of a trial in court is incurred before the Master and to this is added a Master's fee, often amounting to several hundred dollars.

The only thing really accomplished by the Master is the taking of the testimony in writing. This could as well be done in the form of depositions. To accomplish this before the Master, months and sometimes years are consumed. Most of this large expense would be saved if the trial occurred before the court where the case is brought. The Master's services are often more of a clog than an aid in the trial of the case, for the whole matter must be gone over before the court that refers it.

Sometimes the Master is a competent lawyer but frequently not. He is not elected by the people nor is he selected by the parties. His appointment is usually made by the judge at the request of some prominent politician or political clique and he depends upon fees for his compensation. He therefore cannot be expected to discourage any practice that tends to increase his pay. He fixes in the first in stance the amount of his compensation subject to review by the judge and of course is never mean to himself.

Lawyers may disapprove his charges but they dislike such contests and clients pay if they can and if they cannot they are prevented from getting redress. The lawyers also suffer from this practice. So numerous are the causes that produce delays, postponements and adjournments of the case on hearing before the Master, so many and various the notices to be served, chores to be done and red tape and rigamarole to be gone through with, arguing and reviewing objections, pre paring and presenting exceptions, and such like, that an incredible amount of time is wasted for which the lawyer cannot claim compensation. The cases in which such references are necessary are rare and this practice should either be curtailed or abandoned entirely.

THE VERBATIM REPORT ABUSE.

Another incumbrance that has lately been hung to the neck of the Goddess of Justice is the practice of making verbatim reports of everything that is said or done in the trial and bundling it unassorted into a bill of exceptions, and thus making it a part of the record of the case and then requiring a copy of this record to be transcribed and sent to the reviewing court.

The court of review requires all the proceedings to be abstracted and is not expected to examine the transcript. No reason can be shown why this abstract should not be made up and put into the bill of exceptions instead of the verbatim report. Before the days of shorthand reporters this was done, and the unsuccessful party saved the great expense caused first by the transcript of the shorthand reporter and second by the transcript of the Clerk of the Court.

The wise stenographer may be relied upon to report everything that he thinks he can get paid for. Many of the idle remarks and vaporings of the court and counsel and even the speeches are inserted in his report and the unfortunate suitor is usually required to pay fifty cents per page for this effervescence, of no value to him in the further progress of the case. This practice has become so well established that lawyers who oppose it and attempt to make the record in the old way to save their clients becoming victims to such extraordinary charges, meet with discouragement on every hand.

The reporter, the clerk of the court and even the judge will make the path as rocky and full of difficulties as they can. This grievance calls loudly for reform. Why should not the original record made up in the first trial containing the substance of what is done be transported to each reviewing court and returned when the upper courts are done with it? This would give the poor as well as the rich an opportunity to apply to the upper courts for redress.

THE SUPPER ABUSE.

The custom has lately arisen of calling upon the parties to contribute money to pay for meals for the jury.

After the jury has retired, the thrifty bailiff in charge calls the attorneys in the case together and asks them to make up a purse to buy supper for the jury. The effect of a refusal is not known. Each side gives half of the necessary money more or less reluctantly. In some cases the judge has suggested such contributions and of course no one dares to refuse the suggestion and the imposition is permitted. The amount appears small where the litigant has means, but it is too large to be filched in that way, and often is a burden to the poor suitor.

THE EXPERT WITNESS.

Another great incumbrance has fastened to the blind goddess in the shape of the expert witness. The court and jury are sometimes asked to form opinions on questions of science, art, or of value or some other matter about which people generally are not familiar. A rule has been adopted which permits persons who are experts in the particular branch to swear to their opinions as evidence. Here is opened the harvest field of the professional expert witness who is able to demand large fees for testifying to his opinion. Under the circumstances the actual value of his evidence is its market value.

In such contests the wealthy suitor may employ a large number of trained experts who will argue the case in his favor from the witness stand with more force and as much zeal as the lawyer he has employed. The poor man, unable to employ such experts, must see his case slaughtered by these hired witnesses. There should be a narrow limit to this kind of testimony and where it is actually required to enlighten the court or jury, the experts should be persons not related to or acquainted with or employed by either party. They should be selected by the court and a reasonable fee taxed as a part of the cost of the case.

THE LIMITED ARGUMENT ABUSE.

In some states judges are permitted to limit the argument of attorneys to juries, and this privilege is often abused. The writer has sometimes been allowed only twenty minutes to make the opening and closing addresses in cases where several days had been consumed in taking the evidence. Every lawyer has had frequent cause to complain.

Many of the judges who assume to fix the time necessary for an address of this nature have had no experience as advocates and might not be able to make a creditable argument if given all the time in the calendar, yet they assume to determine the period necessary for such an address, and compel the lawyer of long experience, who is the best judge of what is necessary to be said, to cramp his argument into such narrow bounds as to make it unintelligible and to suffer the embarrassment of being compelled to talk by the clock.

The courts of last resort have sometimes set aside judgments because of an abuse by the trial court of this power, but this rarely affords a remedy. It is true that counsel may consume unnecessary time in argument, and it is proper that useless repetitions and remarks not germane to the case be prevented by the court, but a time limit should rarely be put upon the addresses of the lawyers, and where it is the time allowed should be clearly adequate. I contend that bounds should be placed upon the power of judges in this particular so that at least one hour be given for the argument of every case where the amount involved is not less than five hundred dollars.

THE MOTION ABUSE.

From time immemorial it has been customary for all motions to be heard by the judges in person while sitting in open court. When these motions were few and the court had but little business, this practice was unimportant, but with the great increase of court work and the large number of judges engaged in trying cases, this practice, especially in the cities has become a very serious matter. Where a motion is not contested and the party making it is entitled to have it granted as a matter of course, any scrivener can as well enter the order as the judge.

No reason is discoverable why such motions may not be left with such a clerk and the order entered when he reaches it and thus save the loss of time to attorneys in attending before the court waiting their turn and the time of the judge for contested matters. It ought not to be necessary to use a cannon to kill a grass hopper. Where the opposite party desires to contest a motion, he should be required to file his reasons in writing, to which the moving party should reply in a similar manner and then the contest be assigned to the judge to be disposed of without the presence of the attorneys.

THE OFFICIAL FUNERAL.

This is yearly assuming greater importance. In an early day when court business was small, judges few, and deaths were consequently infrequent among members of the bench and high officials of the government, the practice was adopted of adjourning court on account of such deaths, and of suspending court proceedings on the day of funerals. Since then the number of these officials has increased and court business has become so great the dockets of the courts are overcrowded, and suitors subjected to intolerable delays.

Accordingly, this practice of adjourning courts has become a serious matter in its effect upon the public. Not only is it deprived of the services of the judges and their clerks, bailiffs and assistants, but many suitors suffer much loss and inconvenience by having their trials interrupted or postponed. It is probable that every such adjournment in Cook County, participated in by at least twenty judges, causes a loss of more than five thousand dollars, provided the time of judges, court employees, attorneys and their employees, parties, stenographers and witnesses thus affected be taken into consideration.

The question may well be asked, why should Jim Jones, who has never held an office and is not acquainted with John Smith, be compelled to suffer a financial loss on account of the death and burial of the said Smith, when Smith would not be subjected to the same loss by Jones? Only a portion of those who suspend business for this purpose attend the obsequies. The mark of respect has become perfunctory and formal, and the loss and inconvenience entailed upon the public thereby would seem in most instances to be unnecessary and unjust.

CHAPTER XII.

General Qualifications.

In the foregoing chapters I show by illustrations some of the traits which a judge should and should not have. I have not at tempted to enumerate all. The occupant of the bench may have the integrity, intelligence, and good temper necessary to discharge his functions, but should add the experience required to make him an expert in identifying the law.

He should have such familiarity with law books and the collateral doctrines in the minds of the authors that he can understand the precise meaning of what he reads and know when he has made a full investigation and obtained an accurate knowledge of the state of law on the subject under consideration. The law may be likened unto a fluctuating body, such as a flowing stream. It is ever changing and the most important thing to know is the last decision.

Many errors are made by the judge in mistaking the limits of his knowledge. If he assumes to know what he does not he leans upon a broken reed, whereas if he doubts his knowledge unnecessarily he merely loses the time required for verification. The wisdom which sets safe limits to its assumptions and resolves the doubts in favor of ignorance will be most useful in the decision of questions of law. This comes only from experience. An inexperienced person reaches conclusions with slight information, and when reached his mind clicks like a hand cuff, and it is hard to get the key that will un lock it. The less he knows the more he thinks he knows, and the greater the tenacity with which he clings to his opinion.

In some states the laity are elected judges of the highest courts, but have sitting with them lawyers by whom they are controlled and guided in their decisions. There are those who think requiring legal knowledge in a judge gives the profession of law undue power in the government. I see no way of escape from this requirement if we are to have a competent judiciary. A system of surgery which selects persons to perform operations who have no knowledge of the human body would be condemned at once. As essential as knowledge of anatomy is to the surgeon, is knowledge of law to the judge. Without this expert knowledge he is incapable of administering legal justice. Every proposition that comes before him needs to be discussed until he can assume that he has been made competent to guess at the law. So numerous and complicated are the questions which can be raised under our system of jurisprudence that the trial of a suit by such a judge becomes an interminable task.

The grouping together of a large number of facts in the mind requires a trained intellect. This power can only come from experience. No man is born with it. There is no place it can be acquired more effectually by a lawyer than in the conduct of the trial of important cases and in giving counsel in complicated controversies. The danger in making an error in judgment cannot be so fully realized anywhere else. From hard-fought battles and bitter de feats is born that peculiar caution which qualifies the lawyer to gather all facts that are attainable before coming to a conclusion.

So long as we have our present complicated system of jurisprudence, no man who is without this training can be so fully equipped for the bench as the one who has. The college teacher of law may have as much learning and even a wider range of intellectual reading than the trial lawyer, but the importance of examining the last reported case, and of observing the precise point to be decided and the necessity of exploring to the fullest extent the memories of the witnesses for all the details relating to the facts in controversy, may not come with such force and effect to the scholastic lawyer as to the experienced trial advocate.

I therefore contend that candidates for the bench should have at least ten years' practical experience in the trial of lawsuits at the bar before undertaking the judicial office.

Another power of the utmost importance to a judge is the ability to suspend judgment until each party has had full opportunity to be heard. This is the rarest quality of intellect possessed by the human species. It comes as a flower only to the wisest and best. The most difficult thing in this world for even the wise man to do is to wait until he has heard both sides before making up his mind, and then after reaching a conclusion be able to change his opinion, if by the aid of new light it becomes apparent that it ought to be changed.

The judge must assume to know some law and be familiar with some facts in reaching a judgment. He should first ascertain just what propositions of law and fact are in dispute and focus his attention upon these, keeping his mind suspended while eagerly seeking for lighten all sides, until he has procured from each party all the information they can furnish.

If he can do this under all circumstances he will be successful, and if he conducts himself in such a way as to win the confidence of those who come before him he will be an ideal judge. Also it would be well for the candidate to have other experience besides that of a lawyer, that he may have an opportunity to show the public he possesses the essential qualifications. Service as a legislator, or as a member of Congress, or even as a member of a city council, will give him this opportunity. His contact with other men having equal rights with himself will tend to reduce some of the hummocks of conceit likely to develop on a successful lawyer.

It will teach him that notwithstanding his expert knowledge, there is hardly a field where he may not gain some information. The importance of possessing the qualifications I have herein pointed out is often overlooked. One holding a license to practice law is often considered competent for a judicial position with out reference to his previous experience. This office has been used as a reward for military and political service, as an heirloom from father to son, or as a boon to needy relations.

There are sufficient places for rewarding persons who have served the public meritoriously without so misusing the bench. It is unkind to unfit per sons to place them in positions where they must perpetually make an indecent exposure of their incompetency. It is much cheaper and more humane for the country to pension its heroes than to place them in positions for which they are unfitted by education and experience.

Men under forty years of age usually lack experience and knowledge in legal matters sufficient for such an office, and the placing of them on the bench is likely to develop a self-conceit which seriously impairs their usefulness and annoys others who have business with them. Men older than seventy years of age are usually unfit for this office on account of the decline of their powers and the development of a dis position to be garrulous and reminiscent. The old man, who has already spent years in service on the bench, may continue a tolerably good judge until his powers have badly waned, but it is usually difficult for a man of seventy to begin such a career, for then he is likely not to be able to accommodate himself to the needs of a new position.

The atrocious judges of the world, the cruel and heartless tyrants on the bench, were usually elevated to the position in youth, and most of their acts of cruelty were committed before they had reached forty. The senile and decrepit judges elevated to the bench late in life have usually been pliant tools of those who caused their elevation.

This office-should be held by men who have been qualified by education and experience and who still possess some of the vigor, alertness and courage of manhood's prime. It may be impracticable to inspect closely the morals of a candidate for the bench, but it is certain he should not be addicted to the habits which violate the laws or be interested in any illegal business. Gamblers, sports, and persons interested in illicit business or in property used for illegal purposes are unfit.

They are interested against the state and would adorn the prisoner's box better than the bench. The promoters of illegal combinations and stockholders in concerns that are constantly contriving to violate and evade the law are likewise disqualified. Men who are so en tangled with debt as to be in constant vexation regarding their financial affairs should extricate themselves and be able to do private justice before assuming to administer justice for the public. This is said without any disposition to blame those who have been unwise or unfortunate.

Every man will doubtless have a sufficient excuse for his peculiar habits of life. But in the order of the universe there is a place for everything, and it is a part of wisdom to put everything in its place. The peculiar qualities necessary for the use of the judge should be possessed by the candidate. No man is worthy of an official position who does not place the interests of his country higher than his individual prosperity.

No government can long endure whose citizens in and out of office are not ready to sacrifice their own interests, if necessary, to save and preserve it. No man can claim to be a patriot who seeks to procure an office for which he knows he is unfitted, for thereby he sells his country for his own private gain.

In no department can the unfit do a greater injury than in the judicial. It there fore partakes of the nature of treason when any individual or combination strives to place upon the bench men who are incompetent. This government will never be overthrown from without. If it shall perish the cause will come from within, and one of its chief agencies be the placing of corrupt and incompetent men in possession of the scales of justice. Let no one therefore who is a friend of the republic or the lover of justice make the mistake of supporting unfit candidates for the bench.

CHAPTER XIII.

Justinian B. Fair.

Years ago in a city which shall be nameless, a new-born babe was found in a dry goods box by two policemen. It was wrapped in a ragged bed quilt and was slowly bleeding to death. This babe was uncommonly ugly. It had a hair-lip, a withered foot, and its countenance was badly deformed. One said: "Better let the brat die." The other said: "Let's be fair; give it a chance." They took it to the county hospital, where it was cared for until it was sent to the Home for the Friendless.

As the boy grew up his distorted features and deformed body made him a mark for cruel gibes. When he reached ten years he had a bone disease. This kept him on his back near death's door for many months. He suffered the most excruciating agony and finally convalesced, a hunchback. As he went about with his neck bent forward he was a sight so hideous that none of the other children cared to play with him. He was nicknamed "Hunchy."

He would wander into the park and sit under a tree through the long summer days and watch the insects. He made calculations upon their motions. The industry of the ants entertained him. He liked to watch the neatness, skill, and accuracy with which they performed their daily tasks. He noticed every bug had a purpose in each motion which it made.

There came to this park many boys and young men to play baseball. He often watched the game and was much interested and became familiar with its rules. One day when without an umpire someone seeing "Hunchy" suggested in a jocular manner that he be made the umpire for the game. The joke was relished. "Hunchy" was invited and he accepted. All were surprised at his knowledge of the game and the fairness and celerity with which he umpired it. After that his services were in demand as an umpire, he became known to the leagues, and obtained a wide reputation as an umpire in such games. In this way 'he acquired and saved some money. When he had reached the age of twenty-five years the office of justice of the peace, in an outlying suburb, was offered him. The business at that place was so poor no lawyer wanted the position. He accepted it and began the study of law. had no preliminary education except such as had been afforded him at the Home for the Friendless and what he had acquired at odd times. But he was of a studious nature, and had improved every opportunity. He must have a name; the policemen who found and saved him gave him the name of B. Fair because of the remark made when he was so found, and from the judicial fairness he exhibited as an umpire the college boys dubbed him Justinian. In this manner he became entitled to the name of Justinian B. Fair, which was the name used in his election to office.

In the conduct of his court he showed a most earnest desire to arrive at the truth. His long suffering when a lad had given him the grace of patience, and his deformity the virtue of humility. He was honest by nature. He was never tempted by any reward or advantage to himself to favor either side of the controversy. He had an ambition to be a just judge, and to this ideal he consecrated his life. When rendering his decisions his uncomely features, illumined by the soul within, were so transfigured that people forgot his deformity. A lady who was present when he delivered a decision in her favor, on a case where she had long been the victim of oppression, remarked as she left the court-room that Judge Fair had the most beautiful face that she had ever seen.

The business of his court grew very rapidly. People went out of their way to get their causes before him. His fame increased, until finally, through the influence of others, he was placed in an office in the more central part of the city. A few years later he was elected to the nisi prius bench. Here he served with such fidelity and showed such ability as a lawyer and judge that in a few years he was placed upon the Supreme bench of his state. He had no political pull, but was selected because one of the parties desired credit for the election of such a just man to the bench.

Before this Supreme Court there frequently came political questions and the court divided according to politics. Judge Fair was some times relied upon to hold the balance of power. He became generally recognized as one who could not be swayed from the truth and the law by any personal interest, or by the power of any party combination. When a contest arose between powerful corporations and great labor organizations, that threatened anarchy and revolution, he was the only person who could be agreed upon to arbitrate the differences. So well did he discharge this duty that it caused his appointment to the highest court in the nation. There he sat before the eyes of the world, and his skill, learning and fairness attracted the admiration of all mankind.

While holding the office of justice of the peace he became acquainted with a girl who had the psychic power to see through his de formed exterior the matchless beauty of his soul. The union which followed was a happy one. She shared the ambition of her husband and assisted him in every way to get the education which would enable him to perform his life work. When a young man an operation upon his lip was successful in erasing much of its deformity. The withered foot presented him by nature was so skillfully treated by braces and manipulations that he was enabled to walk without crutches, and the lameness caused thereby became scarcely noticeable. By careful observance of the laws of health he gradually overcame much of the weakness of his digestive organs, so that he was seldom dis abled from that cause. The constant doing of good deeds and the harboring of kind and just thoughts, together with the cultivation of his mind, greatly transformed his features, and when he had reached his prime, notwithstanding his hunchback, his noble countenance made him unusually attractive.

By concentrating his efforts to his profession, he had acquired greater learning in legal matters than any of the judges who sat with him. His disposition was merry, but not frivolous, kind but not gushing, generous but not profligate. He was precise and accurate in his observations and dealings. He asked no favors and incurred no unnecessary obligations, and was always punctual in the discharge of duty.

On one occasion, when a motion was made for a new trial based on an alleged error of his own, it was objected by the opposing party that it would take too long to try the case again. To this he remarked: "If I have had time enough to make a mistake, I shall take time enough to correct it." On another occasion, when one of his associates on the bench sought to restrict unduly the argument of an attorney, he said: "The right to be fully heard is as sacred as the right to a just decision." When a person charged with a crime that had be come prevalent was brought before him for sentence, and a great clamor had arisen in the press, demanding that the convicted be made an object lesson to deter others from committing a like offense, the judge refused to listen to the clamor, stating that it was not just that the prisoner at the bar be punished for any offense except the one he had himself committed, and if the fact that others had committed the same offense and were not punished be considered, it should be to mitigate and not to aggravate the punishment. He never fined or threatened to fine any person for contempt of court. Once he said: "I had rather be insulted by two lawyers than have one afraid of me. For," said he, "it is easier to bear the insult than to do without the assistance of an untrammeled lawyer." When asked what qualifications a judge should possess, he said: "A judge should possess the wisdom of Solomon and the patience of Job, the self-denial of a hermit and the industry of an ant, the conscience of a saint and the courage of a martyr."

The following are a few of his epigrammatic utterances:

"A question accurately stated is half decided."

"'A late bench makes a laggard bar."

"Flattery is the most effective bribe."

"Self-conceit is the eclipse that clouds the judicial light."

"Who has too high an opinion of himself has too low an estimate of others."

"A good man stammers more in telling the truth than a rogue in lying."

"The witness who remembers too little is more credible than the one who remembers too much."

"A wise lawyer proves his case by his own witnesses, a foolish one tries to do so by cross-examining his adversary's."

"If a witness has not hurt you, do not try to hurt him."

"Never let a witness know that you doubt his veracity, if you would have him tell the truth."

"The untrained advocate needs the most attention."

"A wise man will learn from a fool, but one fool will not learn from another."

"A good conscience is the compass by which a judge should be guided."

"A good man will not impute worse motives than he would have entertained under the same circumstances, and a bad man is not likely to impute better."

"A single fact outweighs a volume of argument."

Finally the time came for Judge Fair to quit the bench because of advanced age. Full of honors he retired glad to spend his days in domestic quiet with his wife and children. But a controversy arose between two of the greatest nations of the earth, who allied with them on their opposing sides the other great powers. The world became a military camp. Both of the contestants were engaged in whetting the tools of war. But before fighting began, arbitration was proposed and it was agreed that each select an equal number and the whole ap-point an umpire to cast the deciding vote in the case of a tie. The colleges of the earth had for years spawned forth myri-ads of lawyers. Judges, ex-judges and statesmen were as thick as trees in a forest. But only one man could be found who had the confidence of both parties, and this was Justin-ian B. Fair. He was selected for this mighty position and his breath blew out the torch of war.

In one of the few shrines which a grateful people have erected for the devotion of mankind are deposited the mortal re-mains of this judge. Here, as everywhere, the best survives and most effectually resists the tooth of time.

To be a just judge is a noble ambition, and for its attainment one may well put aside all personal considerations, learn to control his whims and natural prejudices, and treat with loving kindness and gentle courtesy all who come before him. He may thus win as important victories and receive as great blessings from the gratitude of his countrymen as can be ac-quired in any other field of human effort. He may not have the form of an Apollo. Nature may not have endowed him with the mental grasp and versatility of a Gladstone. He may be obliged to contend with poverty, sickness and misfortune; but if he has a clean and honest purpose worthy of his great task, and he consecrates himself to it, he will ultimately be appreciated and loved by a great number of his fellow-citi-zens. As long as the earth shall exist men will continue to love justice as a priceless boon and gladly glorify those who have faithfully striven to promote it.

CHAPTER XIV.

Selection.

It is not enough that we determine the qualities that a judge should possess. We must find the man and put him on the bench. To do this we must leave the upper air and come down to practical politics.

We must deal with things as they exist and not as we would have them. In an ideal state the occupant of the bench would be selected by his fellow-citizens and put there without his personal efforts or connivance. Like the coy and blushing maiden, he would wait to be wooed by the masterful voter and yield with reluctance to the over-persuasion of his fellow-citizens and the call of his country. This ideal state has not yet arrived.

The cases where judges are so selected are too rare to be considered. The public de pends upon the aspirations of individuals for candidates and upon the hustling qualities of the candidates for their election to the bench. The lawyer elected must first select himself. He should ask the question: "Am I by disposition, character, education, and experience fitted to become a just and impartial judge? If he can answer this question in the affirmative, then he is justified in seeking the office and using every honorable means therefor. He should make his qualities and aspirations as widely known as possible and so conduct his campaign that if chosen he can enter the office free from any obligations that may conflict with its duties. If, on the contrary, he cannot give this self-endorsement, he has no right to foist himself upon the people as a candidate. He should first become qualified or seek some position for which he is fitted.

While the public have the right to require that the candidate should honestly believe himself qualified, they cannot safely rely upon this belief. There is too much danger that the candidate will overestimate his own ability. The extreme limit of human culture is an accurate self-estimation, and lawyers seldom reach that limit. The public must have other means of information. How are these to be procured? They may look at the candidate, but none are so skilled as to tell from the outside of a man's skull what there is in it. The candidate may have as large a brain as Daniel Webster, but the knowledge therein cannot be weighed in the hay scales. He may move about with the majesty attributed to mighty Jove and thus indicate the pride of a turkey cock instead of the sublime poise of divine wisdom. None can tell by the looks of a horse how fast he can run, or of a toad how far he can hop, much less can he guess from the appearance of a man how much real knowledge he may have on a particular subject. There is but one-way to discover this secret, and that is to require examinations.

As long as he can keep his mouth shut, an ignorant man may pass for a man of learning. He may even speak occasionally, uttering brief and trite bits of wisdom which he has heard or may have slowly worked out, and enjoy great credit for intelligence, but when upon the stand and required to answer terse and well-directed interrogatories, his mask drops off and we see the bottom of his empty mind.

We require school teachers to show their qualifications in this way. Applicants for some municipal and national government offices are treated likewise. If the man who is to carry the mail must prove his competency by an examination, why should not the aspirant for a position where the need of expert knowledge is so great as on the bench be required to submit to this test? Why should not the law fix the qualifications and establish a board of examiners before whom the candidate should appear and prove his competency?

I do not undertake to point out in detail the scope of the examination. It should be practical and relate not to astro-physics but to those matters with which a judge has to deal. The applicant should also furnish evidence that he has had at least ten years' experience in the actual practice of the law and that he has a good moral character. To prevent this requirement from becoming perfunctory,

I think the applicant should give at least thirty days' public notice of his intention of making the application and permit all persons who desire to contest his fit ness to present a written resistance. I suggest that this board of examiners be appointed by the court of last resort and that its members be persons who have had at least ten years' experience on the bench.

A board thus com posed should be able from such an examination to tell whether the proposed candidate has the requisite educational qualifications and whether he probably has a good moral character. I do not think that many incompetent per sons would apply for such an examination. If all candidates for the bench were thus qualified the voter would only need to determine which of these duly qualified persons were the most desirable.

If, then, the warmest handshaker or candidate with the most bewitching smile, or the most active political hustler was elected, the public service would not suffer.

But there is another quality essential to the judge, which no examiner can detect. It is the ability to withstand temptation. Colonel Ingersoll once said: "The test of character is the use man makes of power." The question whether a judge possesses that something which will ever stand for God and eternal justice against the machinations of all forces that may conspire to sway or corrupt it, can only be determined by trying him.

So subtle, cunning, and insidious are the means often employed to undermine judicial honor that many a man has assumed the position with the best of intententions and has been seduced to his fall. To minimize the injury sustained by the public under such circumstances, the term for which a judge is selected should be short, certainly not to exceed four years, and I think two long enough.

Appointments made for life or good behavior have not justified the hopes of the framers of our federal system. The judges thus selected have not excelled those elected by the people, either in learning or character, and many have so conducted themselves as to cause general distrust and dissatisfaction with the system. Public confidence in the fitness and impartiality of the judge cannot in my opinion be maintained except he be chosen by the popular vote and for a short term and be required to return to the people frequently for a renewal of his power.

When he thus seeks reelection, if confidence is lost, he will be defeated and the public relieved of paying for the services of an official they do not trust. If the people retain in their own hands the power to defeat by their votes the judges who have lost their confidence, there is less danger of revolution from a conflict between the will of the majority and the occupants of the bench. This subject is but remotely connected with the object of this book, and I must content myself with merely throwing out a line.

C

HAPTER XV.

The Bench and the Bar.

In concluding this little volume, I call the attention of my brothers in the legal profession on the bench, and at the bar to the tremendous interests which our nation has necessarily placed in our hands. There can be no government of law that does not depend upon lawyers for its administration. Every officer in the judicial branch, from the justice of the peace to the Supreme Court of the nation, should be a trained lawyer. Every legislative body, from the City Council to the Senate of the United to the Senate of the United States, is composed largely of and controlled by members of our profession.

On the pinnacle of the executive department usually sits a lawyer with lawyers for a cabinet. Such is the case with the chief executives of the states and the mayors of the chief cities. Thus all branches of the government are within the grasp of our profession. In the industrial world lawyers are seated on the thrones of power at the heads of the great corporations, and where they do not occupy the chief places the}- have positions of controlling importance.

No great business enterprise is conducted with out their advice and direction. They sit in the nerve centers of every combination to restrain or promote trade, to propagate religious tenets or distribute alms. No proclamation of war or treaty of peace, no great project either by sea or land, is undertaken without some lawyer gives it control and direction. All property passes every few years through their hands. Men, women and children depend upon them for the protection which the government affords.

When we scan the pages of history we find no occasion to blush for our profession. The names of Demosthenes, Cicero, Burke, Jefferson, Webster, Clay, and Lincoln are a few of the beacon lights that mark the progress of our race in its upward march. In every struggle for human liberty the names of prominent lawyers appear at the top of the roll of honor. Their ashes repose in the most honored shrines that a grateful people have erected to their devoted dead. In those sublime moments when occasions have called for martyrs to the cause of truth and justice, they have ever responded, willingly sacrificing their lives for the benefit of the race.

In the long line of presidents of this republic, that grand galaxy of statesmen, the most splendid aggregation of rulers that the earth has had, among the purest, wisest, and most noble were those taken from our profession. They are the fathers of the republic, its protectors and preservers, its heroes and martyrs, who, in the loftiest and most perilous positions of sacred trust, have won by fidelity, courage, and unselfishness an universal admiration. Not only on the highest peaks of human endeavor before the eyes of the multitude, surrounded by the plaudits of the world, has the lawyer shone with excelling luster.

Go into the damp, dismal dungeons where the poor, friendless, and despised culprit shivers in the shadow of the gallows, with an army of foes, who, frenzied with malice at the atrocity of the charge against him, demand his blood. Who lays aside his personal interests, stifles his own desires and imperils his reputation to espouse the cause of this unfortunate? It is the attorney at law! Valiantly he fights for what he considers the right of the prisoner and if he fights in vain he follows his client's cause even to the gallows and is the last on earth to bid him good-bye.

So great is the trust reposed in our profession and so much does the public depend upon our fidelity that happy indeed is that people wherein the lawyers are worthy, and most un fortunate is that nation where they have be come corrupt and debased. When we look about us and see the wrongs that hold sway, how shall we defend ourselves from the charge that our profession has degenerated?

No criminal trust has ever been created except by aid of lawyers. No municipal or other government has become the prey of thieves and grafters or failed to discharge its high functions except through the agency of our profession. If the laws are unjust, or unjustly administered, we are largely responsible. If tainted and corrupt pleas are urged upon the court, or false claims or defenses brought to trial, members of our profession are at fault. If the agents of nefarious combinations are put on the bench, how shall we acquit ourselves of blame?

The community that has so trusted us has the right to demand that we show the vigilance and fidelity which such a great responsibility requires. All considerations demand that the lawyer should be scrupulously honest. His profession gives a broader survey of human society than any other. He sees into the very heart of the body politic. Who is engaged in administering justice should himself be just. No suit should come to trial until two lawyers have fully investigated it and honestly failed to agree. A real difference of opinion should arise before any court is called upon to try a controversy. At the trial each party should be scrupulous to present the truth as he understands it, desiring only that an honest judge pronounce an un biased judgment on the controversy.

As a bad lawyer makes bad judge, one way for the bar to purify the bench is to purify itself. We should all be interested in having our causes correctly decided. We cannot expect to accomplish this unless we act honestly with the court and each other. If we present no causes we believe to be unjust, use no arguments except those we think are true, and resort to no unfair means to influence the court or to procure special favors, the character of the judiciary will be greatly improved. Better than anyone else the lawyer knows the fitness or unfitness of a candidate for judge. The 'public must depend upon him for this information.

Lawyers should watch diligently the conduct of judges and take steps to investigate the first intimation of misconduct. If they omit this duty it will never be done. The same corruption prevalent in other parts of the public service will eventually install itself in the courts. A loss of confidence in the bar and bench is likely to breed revolution and anarchy. We are the inheritors of a noble system formed and transmitted to us by wise and patriotic men.

It is far from perfect, but it is for us to improve and shape for the better accomplishment of the noble work in tended. The legal profession does not afford so great a field for acquiring wealth as some others, but it gives a larger opportunity for doing good and for developing the intellectual and spiritual faculties. The expert lawyer is nevertheless well paid for his services. If he will manage his affairs with prudence there is no need for him to resort to questionable con duct, lie can be honest and provide himself with the luxuries of life. He has no excuse for being a scoundrel, or for putting up his talents like a slave, upon the auction block, to be sold to the highest bidder. He is disloyal to his country and ungrateful to Providence when he hires himself to help defraud either public or private suitors. By no sophistry can he justify such a course. Even the criminal serves, when done with him, will throw him aside like a piece of tainted meat.

If properly pursued, I know of no vocation more pleasant than that of a lawyer. If he desires no results except those which are just and is content when he discharges his duty, the practice of his profession will be full of pleasant experiences. If, on the contrary, he stultifies his conscience, becomes a partner in fraudulent schemes, trains himself for trickery and deception, is constantly engaged in secreting and trying to keep covered the foul work of knaves to enable them to escape just punishment; if he violates and assists others to violate the laws that he has been educated to respect and to enforce, it is difficult to differentiate him from the common criminal, except in the lack of courage used in commit ting crimes. Such a course must degrade the soul, stupefy the intellect, and make him most unhappy, and at the same time tend to under mine the foundations of the state and bring evils upon mankind forages to come.

The highest type of freedom yet conceived by man depends for its existence upon the powerful arm of an organized government, protecting the weak against the strong, the innocent against the vicious, the simple against the crafty, and affording equal opportunities to all. Such a government must be the creature of law and depend for its existence and administration upon a competent and incorruptible bench, taken from, assisted, and sustained by a learned, progressive, and patriotic bar.

The great growth and prosperity of our country has brought forth problems fraught with as great difficulties and perhaps greater temptations and responsibilities than any presented to our noble ancestors. Never was there greater need for character, foresight, and unwavering zeal in supporting the ideals of the republic. Never were the bench and bar harnessed with greater responsibilities. If we love our country, if we cherish its time-honored institutions, if we appreciate the sacrifices of the brave men who cemented with their blood the foundations of its glory, if we would transmit unimpaired and improved the blessings of liberty to posterity, we must yield to no mean or unworthy impulse and miss no opportunity to strike for justice and against oppression.

It is the dearest hope of the author that this little volume, imperfect as it is, may in some way work for the betterment of the bench and the bar, that the tree of liberty which our fathers have planted shall never lose its verdure, but, nourished by the superior wisdom of coming generations, spread its branches farther and wider until all the nations of the earth find shelter beneath its ample boughs.

See Also

16 Pictures of the Bar, Ironic Mosaic of Legal World

16 Pictures of the Juri, Ironic Mosaic of Legal World.